OLYMPIA

OLYMPIA

THE ARCHAEOLOGICAL SITE
AND THE MUSEUMS

OLYMPIA VIKATOU

Archaeologist

EKDOTIKE ATHENON S.A.

Publisher: Christiana G. Christopoulou
Translation: Myriam Caskey
Art editor: Spyros Karachristos
Photographic research: Georgia Moshovakou
Copy editor: Maria Koursi
Photography: Dimitris Benetos, Elias Georgouleas
DTP: E.Varvakis Co.
Colour reproduction, printing, binding:
Metron S.A. - Ekdotike Hellados

ISBN: 978-960-213-418-4
Copyright © 2006 Ekdotike Athenon S.A.
13, Ippokratous st. Athens 106 79
Printed and bound in Greece

CONTENTS

Watercolour showing picturesque view of
Olympia by C. Rottmann (1834-1835).

INTRODUCTION

Sacred place. Civility, quiet concentration, smiling plain amidst low peaceful hills, protected from the savage north wind, from the hot south wind, and below - the sea, from which flows the moist maritime air, rising up along the valley of the Alpheios. There is no more inspiring place in Greece that can so sweetly and with such persistence encourage peace and reconciliation..

Kazantzakis "Travelling. The landscape of Olympia."

Olympia, the most brilliant, the most revered panhellenic Sanctuary, dedicated to Zeus, father of gods and mankind, is near the western coast of the Peloponnese, in the magic valley of the river Alpheios, "in the most beautiful place in Greece" according to Lysias. Below the Kronion hill, where the little river Kladeos joins the plentiful waters of the mythical river Alpheios, in a place that even now is imbued with Olympic beauty and calm, lies the sacred grove of Olympia, the Altis.

Here Zeus and the other divinities were worshipped. Here the Olympic Games were born; here the great values common to all mankind and the pure ideals of sports and the Olympic spirit saw the light of day. Here, with their goal the high ideal of harmony of body and mind, men learned to compete, following the rules of fair play, for the reward of glory alone. Its symbol was the humble crown (stephane) of wild olive, the "*kotinos*", the victor's prize in the Games. The historical course of the Sanctuary is inextricably bound to the Olympic Games, which were held every four years under the watchful eye of the ruling god, Zeus the Thunderer. Indeed, Olympia owes her uniqueness and her splendour to these Games, which, with their ideals, for more than a thousand years forged generations and generations of Greeks, giving a new dimension to human nature.

Situated at the base of the Kronion hill are the North Baths with their beautiful mosaic floors. Shown here is a mosaic from the west colonnade of the Baths, with a representation of a Triton in a chariot drawn by four hippocamps.

THE ARCHAEOLOGICAL SITE

The myths

Despite her isolation, far from the great centres of ancient Greece, in a little corner of the western Peloponnese in the lands of the Eleians, Olympia soon became the greatest panhellenic religious and athletic centre. Throughout the splendid course of its long history, it developed strong ties both with Magna Graeca in the West and with the East. Indeed the myths of Alpheios and Pelops make this quite evident. Alpheios, a handsome youth, fell passionately in love with the nymph Arethousa, a follower of Artemis, in neighbouring Arcadia. She, however, did not requite his love and she asked Artemis to save her. So the goddess transformed her into a spring in Sicilian Syracuse. Alpheios, in despair because of his unrequited love, asked Zeus to relieve him and the father of the gods pitied him and transformed him into the much sung, "silver swirling" king of the rivers of the Peloponnese. Thus the river flowed into the Ionian sea and the water continued its course to Sicily to unite with the springs of Arethousa and the river god symbolically made his match.

Of great importance among the many local myths is the tale of the mythical hero Pelops. From him comes the name of the Peloponnese, which earlier had been known as Apia, from the white poplar tree "leuke or apios" introduced into Olympia by Herakles on his return from the river Acheron. Others say that the name came from the Argive king Apis. The myth narrates that Oinomaos, son of Ares and king of Pisa, the city that had custody of the sanctuary, had a daughter named Hippodameia. He had received the frightful prophesy that he would be killed by the husband of his daughter. To avoid this wretched ending, Oinomaos organized a chariot race. The contenders for the hand of his daughter were obliged to compete with him in an exhausting race beginning at Olympia and ending in the sanctuary of Poseidon at Isthmia. The victor would marry Hippodameia and become king of Pisa. Oinomaos had decreed this contest with the certainty of victory since Ares had given him invincible winged horses. By stipulating that the victor should kill the loser, he would thus be relieved of the undesirable suitors. Indeed he generously allowed each suitor to start first. He, of course, with his winged horses overtook him on the course and killed him. Thirteen contenders had already lost their lives when Pelops, from far away Lydia, arrived at Olympia. He was the father of Atreus and founder of the sorely afflicted dynasty of Pelopids; he was the son of Tantalos and Poseidon was his protector. So that he could take part in the contest, Poseidon gave him winged horses, with which he was sure to win. In one version of the myth, Myrtilos, son of Hermes and charioteer of Oinomaos, is said to have been bribed by Pelops and Hippodameia, with whom he was in love. He therefore replaced the metal linchpins in the chariot wheels with pins of wax. These melted and the chariot collapsed, entangling Oinomaos in the reins, so that he was killed. After his victory, Pelops killed Myrtilos, so that his bribery would not be discovered, and threw his body into the sea off the east coast of the Peloponnese. From then on this was known as the "Myrtoan" sea. To be cleansed of his deed, he then established games in honour of Zeus, and some consider him to be the founder of the Olympic Games. Hippodameia in turn established the Heraia, running races in honour of Zeus' wife, Hera, protectress of the family and marriage. The contest of Pelops and Oinomaos is depicted in the magnificent sculptural composition of the east pediment of the temple of Zeus.

HISTORICAL DEVELOPMENT OF THE SANCTUARY

Prehistoric times (4300-1100 B.C.)

The history of Olympia goes back into the mists of time. The first traces of settlement appear in the Late Neolithic period (4300 - 3100 B.C.). The tumulus that has been investigated in the lower levels of the Pelopion (2500 B.C.) is Early Helladic in date and the first apsidal and rectangular buildings were erected somewhat later (2150 - 1900 B.C.). At this time there was a small sanctuary on the lower slopes of Mt. Kronos, where prehistoric divinities were worshipped, such as Gaia, Kronos, Eileithyia, Rhea, the Idaian Herakles, Themis, the daimon Sosipoles and the Nymphs; there too Gaia had her time-honoured oracle. Prehistoric buildings have been identified in the general area outside the sanctuary as well.

During Mycenaean times (2nd millennium B.C.), the Aitolians led by Oxylos settled in Elis. They established a small settlement around the Sanctuary, the cemetery of which has been excavated on the hills bordering the Museum. This is the time when the cult of Zeus began and Olympia, once a place of habitation, became a place devoted solely to religion, remaining thus throughout its history. The myth of Pelops and Oinomaos, formed in Mycenaean times, shows that Games were held there as early as that time.

Pelops, the mythical founder of the Games, drives his chariot with Hippodameia beside him. The erotic play of the two doves is a reference to the love of the young pair. Scene on a 5th century B.C. vase (Arezzo, Archaeological Museum).

Geometric Period (10th - 8th century B.C.)

The numerous bronze and clay dedications of Geometric times (figurines, tripods and other objects) provide clear evidence that in this period Olympia was already a very important panhellenic religious centre, even though the Sanctuary was simple in form. There was only one wooded grove, with pine, oak, wild olive, poplar and plane trees: the Altis (sacred woods), without any buildings and enclosed by a low wall or peribolos. Among the trees stood the Pelopion (the precinct of Pelops), the great altar of Zeus, the house of Oinomaos, the Hippodameion (precinct dedicated to Hippodameia) and other smaller altars for the worship of the various divinities. Devotees hung their votive offerings on the branches of trees or left them in front of the altars. The Olympic Games were reorganized during the 8th century B.C. by Iphitos (776 B.C.), king of Elis, the most important city of the Eleians, following a relevant prophecy by the Delphic Oracle. It was then that the Games assumed a panhellenic character. At this same time, Iphitos established the institution of the sacred truce, the cessation of hostilities for the duration of the Games. After this, the two powerful cities of the Eleians, Elis and Pisa embarked on centuries of warfare for control of the Sanctuary, between the periods of truce. In the end, Elis was to win and become the city to organize the Games through to the final days of the institution.

Archaic Period (7th-6th centuries B.C.)

The first important buildings were erected: the temple of Hera, the Bouleuterion (Council House), the Prytaneion and the Treasuries. Valuable votives in the thousands were brought from all over the Greek world to be dedicated in the Sanctuary, which was flourishing at that time. The Stadium was within the Sacred Altis, in front of the great altar of Zeus, thus indicating the sacred character of the Games.

Classical Period (5th-4th centuries B.C.)

The dramatic events taking place in the Greek world at the beginning of the 5th century B.C., especially the victories of the Greeks over the Persians, left their mark on art as well, which now was approaching its zenith. The Sanctuary flourished, completing a period of intensive building activity. The splendid temple of Zeus was erected; so also the rest of the Treasuries, the Metroön (temple dedicated to the mother of the gods), the Workshop of Pheidias, the Theokoleon (priests' dwelling) and the Baths. Existing buildings such as the Bouleuterion and the Prytaneion received additions. Stoas bordered the east and south sides of the Altis. At the beginning of the 5th century B.C., the Stadium was taken outside the sacred area. It was widened and provided with an embankment to meet the new requirements of the times and the larger audience. At the same time, the Hippodrome was constructed. Erected toward the end of the 4th century were the Leonidaion (guest house) and the Philippeion (dedicated by the Macedonian king's family). The peribolos of the Altis was expanded to include two gates on the west and one on the south side. During the 4th century B.C., beside the spare Doric order, the light Ionic and the ornate Corinthian styles also appeared in the Altis.

Hellenistic Period
(end of the 4th - 1st century B.C.)

The erection of monumental buildings, of civic rather than sacred

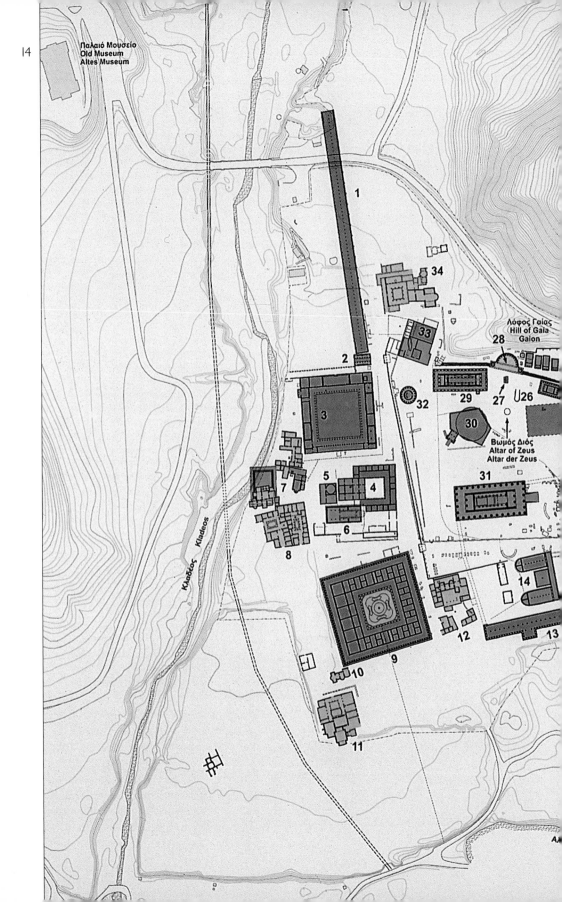

Παλαιό Μουσείο
Old Museum
Altes Museum

1

34

33

Λόφος Γαίας
Hill of Gaia
Gaion

28

2

32

29

27

26

3

30

Βωμός Διός
Altar of Zeus
Altar der Zeus

5

4

31

7

6

8

14

12

13

9

10

11

Κλάδεος Kladeos

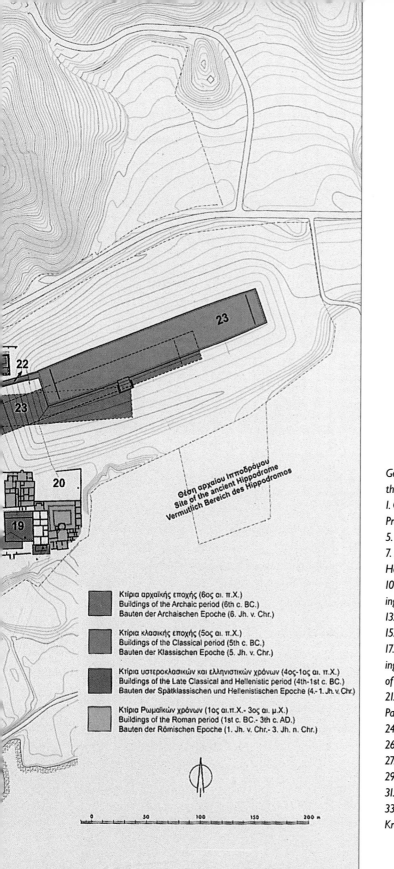

Κτίρια αρχαϊκής εποχής (6ος αι. π.Χ.)
Buildings of the Archaic period (6th c. BC.)
Bauten der Archaischen Epoche (6. Jh. v. Chr.)

Κτίρια κλασικής εποχής (5ος αι. π.Χ.)
Buildings of the Classical period (5th c. BC.)
Bauten der Klassischen Epoche (5. Jh. v. Chr.)

Κτίρια υστεροκλασικών και ελληνιστικών χρόνων (4ος-1ος αι. π.Χ.)
Buildings of the Late Classical and Hellenistic period (4th-1st c. BC.)
Bauten der Spätklassischen und Hellenistischen Epoche (4.-1. Jh. v. Chr.)

Κτίρια Ρωμαϊκών χρόνων (1ος αι.π.Χ.- 3ος αι. μ.Χ.)
Buildings of the Roman period (1st c. BC.- 3th c. AD.)
Bauten der Römischen Epoche (1. Jh. v. Chr.- 3. Jh. n. Chr.)

0 50 100 150 200 m

General topographical plan of the Sanctuary of Olympia.
I. Gymnasium 2. Gymnasium Propylon 3. Palaistra 4. Theekoleon 5. Heroön 6. Workshop of Pheidias 7. Baths of Kladeos 8. Roman Hostels 9. Leonidaion 10. Leonidaion Baths II. SW Building - Athletic Club 12. South Baths 13. South Stoa 14. Bouleuterion 15. Odeion 16. Apse of Nero 17. Sanctuary Hearth 18. SE Building 19. Greek Building (later House of Nero) 20. East Baths - Octagon 21. Echo Stoa 22. Krypte (Hidden Passageway) 23. Stadium 24. The Treasuries 25. Metroön 26. Prehistoric Apsidal Building III 27. Altar of Hera 28. Nymphaion 29. Heraion 30. Pelopion 31. Temple of Zeus 32. Philippeion 33. Prytaneion 34. North Baths or Kronion Baths.

The valley of Olympia before the excavations. At the left the conical Kronion hill (height ca. 123 m.) dominates the north side of the sanctuary (A. Boetticher, Olympia 1886).

character, continued during Hellenistic times. Athletic facilities (Palaistra-Gymnasium) were built next to the Kladeos river to serve the needs of the athletes, who earlier trained on the level space that had existed there. Beside the Olympic victors' statues that stood in the Altis, were added statues and monuments of many rulers and Hellenistic kings, such as Antigonos, Seleukos, Demetrios Poliorketes, Antiochos etc., all striving in this way to proclaim their presence and their power in the Greek world. Among these the monument of Ptolemy and Arsinoe stands out.

Roman Period
(1st century B.C - 4th century A.C.)

With the Roman period the Olympic and competitive spirit of the Games had passed its prime. Yet the building program in the Sanctuary continued with the erection of impressive constructions reflecting the spirit of the times. These included the Nymphaion (monumental springhouse), the Baths, luxurious villas and guesthouses. Despite the ravages of the Roman general Sulla (87 B.C.), the Sanctuary thrived and reached a height of prosperity during the years of Augustus. The 2nd century A.C., when the ancient traveller Pausanias visited Olympia, was a time of revival for both Sanctuary and venerable oracle. At the beginning of the 3rd century A.C., Caracalla (211-217 A.C.) gave the privilege of Roman citizenship to all inhabitants of the Roman empire and the panhellenic Olympic Games became universal.

Slightly later, in A.D. 267, under threat of incursion by the Germanic tribe of Herulians, who did not, however, reach Olympia, a wall was hastily erected to protect the temple of Zeus and the southern part of the Altis. Building material was taken from the Treasuries, the Bouleuterion, the Leonidion, the Metroon, the Echo Stoa and the Propylon of Pelops. The greater part of these buildings was thus destroyed.

Early Christian times - end of the Sanctuary (4th - 7th centuries A.C.)

In A.D. 393, Theodosius I, emperor of Byzantium, brought the Olympic Games to an end by imperial decree. Somewhat later, Theodosius II ordered the monuments to be set on fire (A.D. 426). The ancient Sanctuaries ceased to function. The destruction of the buildings of Olympia was completed by two great earthquakes, one in A.D. 522 and the other in 551. At this time a little rural settlement grew up in the Altis between the temple of Zeus and the Stadium, spreading as far as the Early Christian Basilica, which stood over the ruins of the Workshop of Pheidias. The place was finally abandoned in the 7th century A.C. and gradually buried beneath the earth that slid down from the Kronion hill and the silt left by the flooding of the Alpheios river. The centuries passed while Olympia lay in oblivion, to be rediscovered only in the 19th century when excavations brought to light the splendid monuments and revived the history of the sacred place. The German Archaeological Institute of Athens has continued excavations at intervals up to today. During 2002-2004, as part of an extensive program of conservation of the monuments in the Altis by the Ministry of Culture, all the mosaics in the buildings and the inscriptions on stone received conservation and, in collaboration with the German Archaeological Institute, a difficult and impressive program of restoration was carried out on the temple of Zeus and on the Philippeion.

TOUR OF THE MONUMENTS

Strolling beside the banks of the river through the ancient ruins, broken into pieces by earthquake and by the excesses of mankind,

One of the loveliest creations of ancient Greek architecture is the tholos of Olympia, called the Philippeion after its dedicator, Philip II. Construction of the circular Ionic building began in 338 B.C. The Philippeion is shown here during its restoration.

their extraordinary colours washed and obliterated by the Alpheios, which finally buried them, one can only think how generously this sacred place has been endowed by history and by nature with perpetual glory and beauty. The ruins lie southwest of the Kronion hill, among the trees, with spring-blooming Judas trees (cercis siliquastrum), oleanders and wild flowers, with cyclamen and anemones that spring up everywhere, even from cracks in the ancient blocks. The modern pilgrim to Olympia indeed is offered a unique scene with an extraordinarily rich feast of colour.

In the central part of the Archaeological site is the **Altis**, the main Sanctuary, surrounded by a peribolos wall enclosing the temples, the Treasuries and the Altars. Among these monuments, in antiquity, stood hundreds of statues, bronze and marble dedications that have not survived to modern times. To the east of the Altis lies the Stadium, and to the west are the supplementary buildings: athletic installations (Gymnasium, Palaistra), bathing establishments, hot baths, guest houses, workshops and so on. These are separated from the Altis by the Sacred Way, which cuts through the Sanctuary from N to S.

Going along the Sacred Way, the first building on the left is the **Kronion Baths** or north baths. This is a large building complex of Roman times that was built over a bathing establishment of the

Hellenistic period. It comprises a central reservoir enclosed by a colonnade and many rooms and supplementary areas. The floor of the colonnade is decorated with splendid mosaics (Triton in a chariot drawn by sea horses, a Nereid riding a sea bull and a dolphin) of Roman times. The baths were destroyed by earthquake during the 3rd century A.C., but were then rebuilt and expanded. In the 5th century A.C., the building was used for producing farm products (wine) and as a ceramic workshop.

A little to the south is the **Prytaneion**. This was the seat of the Prytaneis, the officials of the sanctuary who were responsible for the sacrifices made at the altars. This was the central administration of the Sanctuary and the building was among the most important. Its construction began at the end of the 6th/beginning of the 5th century B.C. Initially it was a small square building to which additions were gradually made. The official feasts in honour of the Olympic victors were held in the halls of the north or west sides. An altar of Hestia stood in one of the central rooms; here the sacred fire perpetually burned. At this altar the Eleians made the initial sacrifice on the first day of the Games.

The first building the visitor sees on entering the **Altis** is the **Philippeion**, next to the NW entrance of the sacred temenos. The building took its name from the Macedonian king, Philip II, who dedicated it to Zeus after his victory at Chaironeia in 338 B.C. After the death of Philip, the building was finished by his son, Alexander the Great. It is a circular construction (diam. 15,25 m.) with 18 Ionic exterior columns and 9 engaged columns with Corinthian capitals in

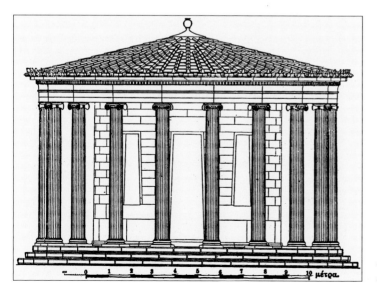

Restoration drawing of the Philippeion (by H. Schleif).

The earliest temple in the Sanctuary, dedicated to Hera, was built around 600 B.C. at the base of the Kronion hill, below the venerable sanctuaries where the prehistoric divinities were worshipped and the most ancient oracle of Ge and her daughter Themis made their prophesies. Shown here is the Heraion from the northeast. To the right can be seen part of the Nymphaion.

the interior. It had an Ionic entablature and a marble roof crowned by a bronze poppy. Inside, opposite the entrance, was a base on which stood five chryselephantine (gold and ivory) statues representing: Alexander, his parents, Philip and Olympias, and the parents of Philip, Amyntas III and Eurydike, works of the famous sculptor Leochares. The Philippeion, the only circular building in the Altis, is considered to be one of the most elegant of ancient buildings. The Macedonian royal family dedicated it in the most splendid of Sanctuaries to show its total domination over the lands of Greece. The impressive program of restoration of the monument was completed in 2005.

East of the **Philippeion** is the **Heraion**, a temple dedicated to the goddess Hera by the inhabitants of Skillous, who were

The notable length of the ground-plan of the temple of Hera is a feature of Doric temples of archaic times. According to one theory, an earlier temple of Hera with pronaos and cella, was built in 650 B.C on this same spot. To this a colonnade and opisthodomos were added in 600 B.C.

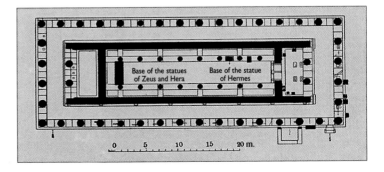

Base of the statues of Zeus and Hera   Base of the statue of Hermes

0   5   10   15   20 m.

allies of the Pisans. Initially it was Zeus who was worshipped here. The temple is one of the earliest examples of monumental temple construction in Greece and it is datable around 600 B.C. It is of the Doric order, with 6 columns along the narrow ends and 16 along the sides (peripteral hexastyle) (50,01 x 18,76 m.). It comprises a pronaos, cella and opisthodomos. The cella is divided into three aisles by two rows of eight Doric columns, with short cross-walls running from every other column to the cella wall, thus forming five small niches on each side. The pronaos and opisthodomos had each two columns between the antae (distyle in antis).

The columns, 5,21 m. in height, were originally of wood, but these were gradually replaced by stone columns. When Pausanias visited Olympia in 170 B.C., there was still one wooden column standing in the opisthodomos of the temple. Since replacement of the columns happened gradually, the new columns, and especially the column capitals, differ from each other as they followed the style of the time when they were made. Thus the temple illustrates the whole development of the Doric style from Archaic to Roman times. Painted portraits of the winners of the Heraia were placed in shallow square hollows in the columns of the colonnade. The lower part of the temple and the columns, as they were replaced, were made of conglomerate. Unfired bricks were used for the upper part of the walls, the entablature was of wood with painted terracotta sheath-

The altar of Hera, where today is lit the Olympic flame that signals the beginning of the modern Olympic Games. Visible in the background is the monumental spring (water system) dedicated to the temple by the benefactor Herodes Atticus and his wife Regilla.

Old restoration sketch of the east façade of the temple of Hera. The goddess Hera was worshipped here as "Olympia", an epithet she inherited from the prehistoric goddess Eileithyia, who gave the name likewise to the site. Hera was the first divinity to have a temple in the Altis.

ing and the roof-tiles were also of clay. A large terracotta disk-akroterion stood on the pedimental apex; it is now in the Archaeological Museum of Olympia (henceforth A.M.O.). At the end of the cella, where a stone pedestal base is still preserved, stood the cult statues of Zeus and Hera. Every 4 years, the 16 noble ladies of Elis who organized the Heraia, wove a new peplos for the goddess and placed it on her cult statue.

Kept in the Heraion was the disk of **Iphitos**, on which were inscribed the terms of the sacred Olympic truce. Here too was another important item, the **Table of Kolotes**, pupil of Pheidias. It was made of gold and ivory and on it were displayed the wreaths of wild olive for crowning the Olympic victors. In the opisthodomos was the **Chest of Kypselos**, dedicated by the descendents of the Corinthian tyrant. It was made of wood, gold and ivory and was decorated with many mythological scenes. For these works, which have not survived, we have Pausanias' valuable and detailed descriptions. The famous statue of **Hermes** by the great sculptor Praxiteles came to light during excavations in the cella. In Roman times the temple was transformed into a sort of Museum in which were kept some of the most valuable votive offerings of the Sanctuary. Statues of noble Elean women stood in the Pronaos.

A little staircase in the NW corner of the temple led to the most ancient **Sanctuary of Gaia** on the southern slopes of the Kronion hill.

In front of the temple stands the stone **Altar of Hera**. Here, today, the Olympic flame is lit, in a ritual that was initiated in 1936 at the Olympic Games of Berlin and it marks the start of the present-day Olympic Games. The sacred flame, symbol of peace and reconciliation among the nations, is lit by the rays of the sun shining through a magnifying glass. Then the procession of priestesses carry the flame to the Stadium, where the first priestess gives it to the first runner to begin the great journey, carrying the message of peace from the cradle of the Olympic ideal to all the world.

South of the Heraion is the **Pelopion**, a temenos dedicated to the hero Pelops. The enormous tumulus (diam. 27 m.) and the stone peribolos wall go back to the EH II period (2500 B.C.) in the lower layers. It is the earliest construction in the Altis. In that early time, some prehistoric divinity, probably of fertility, was evidently worshipped here. Later on the prehistoric tumulus was occupied by the Pelopion. The area was reorganized in the 6th century B.C. and in the 5th century B.C. it was enclosed by a pentagonal peribolos wall with a monumental Doric propylon in the SW side. Trees and statues stood within the temenos in antiquity. Pausanias tells us that each year the officials sacrificed a black ram in the Pelopion temenos in honour of the dead hero.

East of the Pelopion was probably the Hippodameion, a teme-

Erected on the level space south of the Kronion hill were the prehistoric buildings of Olympia. Visible today is Building III with its characteristic apsidal plan. View of the building from the north.

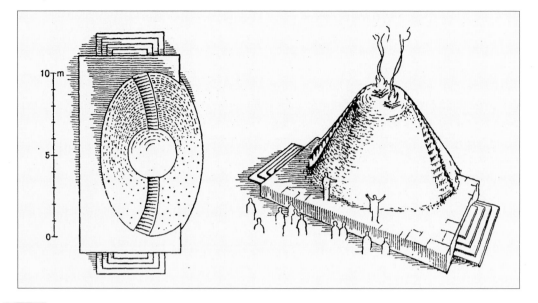

Hypothetical plan and reconstruction of the great altar of Zeus. It is conical, built up of ashes from the animal sacrifices. Following a very ancient liturgical tradition, the Eleians sacrificed on the other 70 altars estimated to have stood in the Altis: once a month, frankincense mixed with flour and honey was burned on olive branches and wine was poured as liquid offering.

nos dedicated to Hippodameia, wife of Pelops. Its exact location has not been found. Probably in this area too was the only wooden column that remained from the House of Oinomaos, which had been destroyed by fire. Pausanias mentions it.

Southeast of the Heraion six prehistoric buildings have been excavated. Visible today is only one, **Building III.** The plan is apsidal and it is datable to the end of the Early Helladic III period (2150-2000 B.C.). Recent research has shown that at that time there were connections with the Cetina culture of the Dalmatian coast. These apsidal buildings and the prehistoric tumulus beneath the Pelopion are the earliest constructions in the Sanctuary. At the time when they were built, prehistoric divinities were worshipped in this place. During the Middle Helladic I period (2000-1900) rectangular buildings were erected above the apsidal constructions. Later on the area was filled in and prepared for the buildings of historic times.

The Great Altar of Zeus, which for centuries was the focus of the cult of the god, probably stood in the area lying to the east of the Pelopion and the Heraion. No trace remains of the altar, but a thick layer of ash spread over a wide area bears witness to its existence. The myth tells us that Zeus himself determined the position of the altar by hurling a thunderbolt from Mt. Olympos. Poplar wood exclusively was used for the sacrifices, as did Herakles when he sacrificed to Zeus. On a krepis around three metres high stood the main altar. It consisted of the ash accumulation from the sacrifices and from the altar of Hestia in the Prytaneion and it was conical in form. The height is estimated to have been 6,50 m. with a circumference of 9,50 m. The sacrifice of the animals took place at the base of the altar on the *prothysis* and the priests then took the legs to the top of the altar where they were burned. Pausanias, who is our source of information for the monument (V 13, 8-11), reports that on the nineteenth day of the month Elaphion (end of March) the ashes were taken from the altar of Hestia in the Prytaneion, mixed with water taken only from the river Alpheios, and the paste then daubed on the surface of the altar. It was destroyed probably during the reigns of the emperors Theodosius I and II.

Northeast of the Heraion is the Nymphaion, the ruins of the water supply system dedicated to the Sanctuary by the patron of the arts Herodes Attikos and his wife Regilla in A.D. 160. Their provision solved the problem of the water supply, which was particularly acute during the Olympic Games. The Nymphaion is a two-storey apsidal construction (diam. 16,62 m.), in front of which were two reservoirs, one semi-circular, one rectangular and differing in height. The walls were faced with polychrome marble. On each floor of the two-storey semicircular wall of the apse there were eleven niches, each decorated with a marble statue. On the top

Restoration drawing of the Nymphaion. The niches in the two-storey semi-circular apse held statues, now exhibited in the Archaeological Museum. (Restoration by R. Bol, Olympische Forschungen XV, Berlin 1984, Beilage 5).

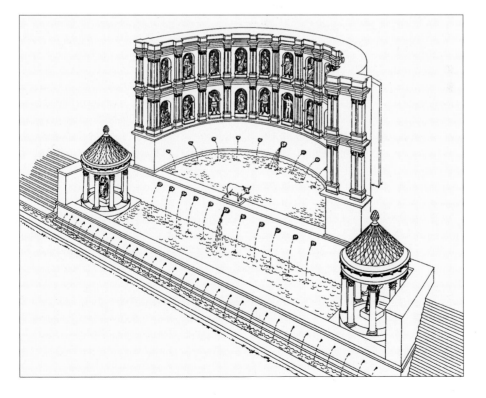

The terrace of the Treasuries. Shown are the Treasury of the Sikyonians and the stepped krepis of the terrace.

Plan of the Treasuries. In the first building (A) were found the foundations of the sanctuary of Eileithyia and the snake-like daimon Sosipoles. Following in a row are the Treasuries of the Sikyonians (B), the Syracusans →

floor were statues of the family of Herodes Attikos and his house; on the bottom, statues of Antoninus Pius and his family. The central niche on each floor held a statue of Zeus. In the middle of the upper reservoir stood a marble bull, symbol of the watery element, dedicated by Regilla. At each end of the rectangular reservoir there was a little circular colonnaded building of the Corinthian order. Each held a statue (of Herodes Attikos and Antoninus Pius or Marcus Aurelius). The reservoirs collected the water that was piped from springs in the hills of the wider area. Through the system, water was circulated in pipes throughout the Sanctuary. Many of the statues from the Nymphaion are displayed in the Archaeological Museum.

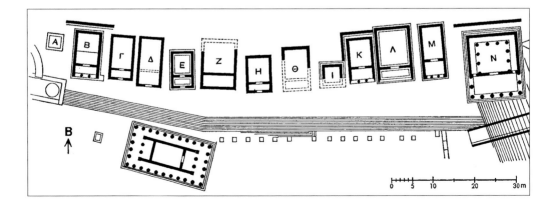

In Archaic times a terrace was constructed on the southern slopes of the Kronion hill, east of the Nymphaion and at a higher level. Here the **Treasuries** were built. They were small buildings in the form of a temple, with cella and pronaos, that were dedicated by various cities to the Sanctuary. Their name comes from the valuable dedications later kept in them. Except for the Treasury of Gela, which was hexastyle, they had a simple façade with two columns in antis (distyle in antis). The ruins of a total of twelve Treasuries remain today, of which only five can be identified with certainty: of the Sikyonians, the Selinountians, the Metapontians, the Megarians and the people of Gela. From Pausanias we know that other Treasuries were dedicated by the Syracusans, the Byzantians, the Sybarites and the Kyrenaians. Most were dedicated by the cities of Magna Graeca (South Italy and Sicily) and are dated in the 6th and 5th centuries B.C. The earliest was the Treasury of the Sikyonians (first from the west), built at the same time as the Heraion. It was dedicated by Sikyon, a city not far from Corinth. By the middle of the 5th century B.C., all the Treasuries had been built. Of special importance are the terracotta entablatures, with the colours preserved in beautiful condition, and the pediment of the Treasury of the Megarians (A.M.O.).

The terrace of the Treasuries is approached by a stone stairway that was constructed in the 4th century B.C. In later years a large supporting wall with buttresses was built behind the Trea-

The Metroön, a little Doric temple dedicated to the Mother of the Gods, was built in the middle of the 4th century B.C. Preserved today are parts of the stylobate and the entablature. View of the building from the NE. Visible in the background are the temple of Zeus, the tumulus of Pelops and the columns of the Heraion.

(Γ), unknown (Δ), the Epidamnians (E), the Byzantians (Z), the Sybarites (H), the Cyrenians (Θ), the altar of Ge (Gaia) (I), the Selinuntines (K), the Metapontines (Λ), the Megarians (M), and the Geloans (N).

Restoration drawing of the Metroön. Visible to the left are some of the Treasuries, and to the right the Propylon of the Krypte (the vaulted passageway to the Stadium) and part of the Echo Stoa (from F. Adler, Olympia II).

suries toward the Kronion. This marked the northern boundary of the Altis.

In front of the terrace of the Treasuries is the **Metroön**, a small Doric temple (20,67 x 10,62 m.) of the 4th century B.C., sacred to Rhea, mother of the gods, known later as Kybele. It had 6 columns on the ends and 11 on the long sides and comprised a pronaos, cella and opisthodomos. In Roman times it was used for the worship of the Roman emperors, whose statues stood in the cella. Here too was found the torso of an over life-sized statue of Augustus (A.M.O.).

At the foot of the terrace of the Treasuries, along the road that led to the Stadium, stood the **Zanes**, bronze statues of Zeus paid for by the fines levied on athletes who had broken the rules of the Games. Carved on the statue bases was an inscription exhorting the athletes to rely on their own bodily prowess for an Olympic victory rather than resorting to fraud. At the end was written the name of the athlete. The Zanes were placed before the entrance to the Stadium in a conspicuous place as an example to those competing in the Games. Pausanias recounts all the punishments of the athletes. The first six Zanes were made during the 98th Olympiad (388 B.C.) from the fine imposed on the Thessalian boxer Eupolos for having bribed three of his fellow athletes. In the 112th Olympiad (332 B.C.), the Athenian pentathlon athlete Kallippos was penalized

The stone bases of the Zanes
stand along the krepis of
the Treasuries, in front of the
entrance to the Stadium.
On one of these is preserved the
inscription of the sculptor Kleon:
ΚΛΕΩΝ ΣΙΚΥΩΝΙΟΣ ΕΠΟΙ...
(Kleon the Sikyonian made...).
In the background the entrance
to the Stadium.

General view of the Krypte and
the Stadium from the west. The
vaulted entrance to the Stadium
was known as the "Krypte"
because the vault was covered
over with an introduced fill
and therefore hidden.

General view of the Stadium from the west. Visible on the south embankment (right) is the Exedra of the Hellanodikai, and on the north embankment (left) the stone altar of Demeter Chamyne. The spectators sat on the ground of the embankments to watch the Games.

for bribery and had to put up six Zanes. Finally, in the 201st Olympiad (A.D. 25), the penalty imposed on the Alexandrian pancratiast Sarapion is extraordinary, for it was not for breaking the rules but for cowardice. It is worth noting that from the 4th century B.C. on, penalties were imposed when conventional ethical values were denied, thus affecting the athletic ideal of the Games.

The entrance to the **Stadium**, where the Olympic Games took place, was, as it is today, through the **Krypte,** the hidden entrance, which was built in Hellenistic times (3rd century B.C.). This is a vaulted passageway with a Corinthian propylon at the west end that was added in Roman times. At each side of the entrance stood a statue of Nemesis/Tyche, now on display in the Museum of the History of the Olympic Games in Antiquity (henceforth M.H.O.A.). Athletes, judges, officials and priests entered the Stadium through the Krypte, whereas the audience entered from the embankments.

The Stadium seen today by the visitor is the third in a series and is dated in the 5th century B.C. The two previous stadia, of archaic times, were in the Altis. Stadium I, dated at the beginning of the 6th century B.C., ran along the terrace of the Treasuries. It was simply a level space, without embankments for seating, with its west end towards the Altar of Zeus, where the athletes ended their course. The earliest Stadium was probably in the same place, since from 776

B.C. on the Games were held without a break. Toward the end of the 6th century B.C., it was shifted slightly to the east and embankments were built up along the long sides for the audience (Stadium II). The location of the archaic stadia within the Altis bears witness to the religious character of the Games.

At the beginning of the 5th century, when the Games had reached their zenith, the Stadium took on its final form. The continually increasing numbers of athletes participating and the corresponding increase in size of the audience from everywhere in the world, meant that a larger Stadium had to be built. The athletic track was moved 82 m. further east and 7 m. to the north, and embankments were raised on all sides (Stadium III). Around the middle of the 4th century B.C., when the Echo Colonnade or Stoa was built, the Stadium was finally removed from the Sacred Altis. The event was a reflection of the times, for the Games were now primarily athletic and mundane rather than religious.

The Stadium track is 212,54 m. in length and 28,50 m. wide. The distance between the two stone starting and finishing posts is 192,27 m., or 600 Olympic feet (1 foot = 32,04 m.). The starting point is marked by the *balbis* (rope drawn across the starting point) at the east, and the finish by that at the west end of the Stadium. In the north bank there is an altar of Roman times to the goddess Demeter Chamyne. Her priestess stood here during the Games. In the south embankment a stone exedra, still preserved, provided seats for the Hellanodikai or umpires. The Stadium had a seating capacity of some 40,000 - 45,000. Spectators sat directly on the

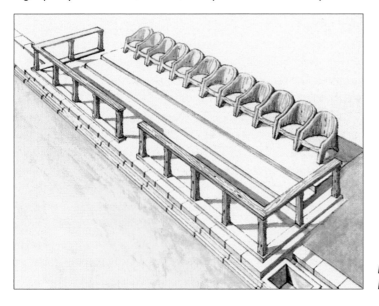

Reconstruction drawing of the Exedra of the Hellanodikai.

Hypothetical restoration of the Hippodrome (Drawing by K. Iliakis, archive of Ekdotike Athenon). At the left are the Stoa of Agnaptos and the starting mechanism, which was the most impressive feature of the Hippodrome.

ground. The few existing stone seats in the Stadium were honourary seats for officials. It was probably in Roman times that wooden seats were constructed on the embankments and repairs were carried out. Around the track is a stone drain with small basins at intervals for run-off from the banks. In addition to the Olympic Games, the Heraia too were held in the Stadium. Many finds have come from the excavations in the Stadia, especially bronzes, that were found in wells dug as early as Archaic times to provide the audience with sufficient water. When these went out of use they served as dumps.

Along the south side of the Stadium was the **Hippodrome,** a grand construction of the 5th century B.C., with embankments for the spectators. Here were held the riding contests and the chariot races. The track, or *dromos,* of the Hippodrome, elliptical in plan, was some 780 m. long and about 320 m. wide. At about the centre of the length of the course was a wooden, or perhaps stone, divider around which ran the contestants. There was a complicated and impressive starting system for the horses (*hippaphesis*), invented by the portrait sculptor, Kleoitas. The hippaphesis was triangular in form, like the prow of a ship. In the angle, "at the point of the ram", a tall pole crowned by a bronze dolphin was placed. The horses and chariots took their places along the sides of the triangle in special stalls. On an altar in the middle of the prow stood a bronze eagle, which was raised by a mechanism within the altar so that it was visible to all the spectators. At the same time the dolphin was lowered into the earth. At this point, the ropes in front of the stalls with the horses were withdrawn in stages and the race began. The Hippodrome was bordered at the end toward the Altis by the Stoa of Agnaptos. Near the starting point was a statue of Hippodameia and at its SE corner was a little altar dedicated to Taraxippos, a divinity who caused the horses to panic. The entire monumental construction may well have been washed away by the river Alpheios, and this may explain why it has never been found. Pausanias gives us a full description (Elis II, xx.10 ff.).

The Echo Stoa (98 x 12,5 m.) was built around 350 B.C. to separate the Stadium from the Altis of which it formed the eastern boundary. The exterior colonnade was Doric and the interior Corinthian. Its name came from the sevenfold echo that was a characteristic of the acoustics of the building. It was also known as the "Stoa Poikile" from the painted decoration of the interior. In the middle of the 3rd century B.C., the monument of Ptolemy II Philadelpheus and Arsinoe was erected in front of the Stoa. The official statues of the pair stood on two tall Ionic columns (H. 8,89 m.) that rested on a stone *krepis* or platform. Preserved today are only the stone krepis and fragments of the Ionic columns. Bases found along the length of the façade show that other dedications too were placed in front of the Stoa.

In the SE part of the Altis was the Sanctuary of Hestia of the Pisans, known now as the **Southeast building.** It was built in the 5th century B.C., functioning as it was until the 4th century B.C. when the building was altered. Its place was taken in the 1st century A.C. (A.D. 65-67) by an impressive building complex with a central peristyle, atrium, courtyards, gardens, rooms and so forth. This was the **Villa of Nero,** built expressly for the emperor's visit when he came to Olympia to take part in the Games and was proclaimed an Olympic victor. The building in turn was covered over in

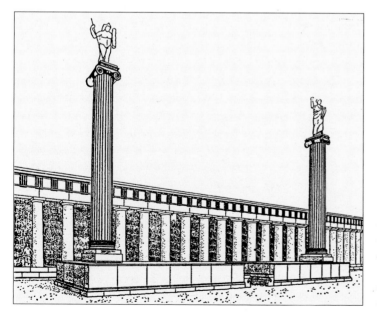

Reconstruction drawing of the monument of Ptolemy II and Arsinoe (by W. Hoepfner, AM Beih. I, 1971). Gilded statues of the king and his wife stood on two tall Ionic columns.

The Echo Stoa was built in the middle of the 4th century B.C. It formed the boundary of the east side of the Altis and separated the athletic area (Stadium) from the sacred. Shown here are building remains of the Stoa and part of an Ionic column from the monument of Ptolemy II and Arsinoe.

the 3rd century A.C. by the **East Baths**. The best preserved part is at the SE corner, known as the "Octagon" because of the form of its central room. The impressive mosaic floor, with sea creatures, is preserved in excellent condition. The remains of a small **Odeion** of Roman times are preserved in the SW part of the complex together with the foundations of the celebrated **Apse of Nero**, which formed the main entrance to the Street of the Festivals south of the Temple of Zeus.

The enormous **Temple of Zeus** stood in a conspicuous place at the centre of the Altis. It was erected from the spoils of battles won by the Eleians during the Triphylian wars. Its construction began in 470 B.C. and was completed in 456 B.C. with Libon the Eleian as architect. This is the largest temple in the Peloponnese and it was considered as a "canon", the perfect expression of the Doric temple. The building material, as with most buildings in the Sanctuary, is the local conglomerate (containing shells). It was transported there by raft on the Alpheios, which at that time was navigable. The ancient quarry has been found 14 km. east of Olympia at the modern village of Louvros. A white marble stucco was applied to the surfaces of walls and columns. The pedimental sculpture, tiles and lion-head spouts were of marble.

The temple is oriented E-W and it is peripteral, with 6 columns on the ends and 13 on the long sides (64,12 x 27,68 m.). The columns were 10,43 m. high with a lower diameter of 2,25 m. The columns supported a splendid Doric entablature with architrave, Doric frieze (triglyphs and metopes), pediment, geison and akroteria. The total elevation of the temple is estimated to have been 20,25 m. The plan of the temple comprises pronaos, cella and opisthodomos. Both pronaos and opisthodomos are distyle in antis. The preserved floor of the pronaos, with a scene of Tritons, is Hellenistic. The cella is divided into three aisles by two rows of two-tiered colonnades, each row with seven Doric columns. At the end of the central aisle or nave was the chryselephantine statue of Zeus, made by the great sculptor Pheidias and considered one of the seven wonders of the ancient world. Wooden stairways led from the side aisles to galleries above, where the statue could be viewed from close-up. With the final abolishing of the Olympic Games, the colossal statue was taken to Constantinople where it was destroyed by fire around A.D. 475.

The temple had splendid pedimental compositions, with fine examples of the severe style in sculpture, now on exhibit in the Archaeological Museum. The east pediment shows the chariot race between Pelops and Oinomaos. Represented in the west pediment is the battle between the Lapiths and Centaurs. Twelve metopes, above the entrance to the pronaos and the opisthodomos, complete the sculptural decoration of the building with the labours of Herakles. The outer metopes of the colon-

The Octagon was part of the East Baths and it is one of the best preserved monuments in the Altis. General view of the Octagon from the northwest.

The temple of Zeus from the east. Construction of the imposing temple of Zeus in the middle of the Altis began in 470 B.C. In order to raise it above all the other buildings in the Sanctuary, it was placed on a high krepis (3 m.). It was designed by the local architect, Libon. Preserved are the foundations and many of the architectural members, which lie around it.

nades were undecorated. In A.D. 146, 21 gilded bronze shields were hung on these, as a dedication to the temple by the Roman commander Mummius in memory of his victory over the Greeks at the Isthmos (destruction of Corinth). A gilded Nike, by the sculptor Paionios, was the central akroterion of the east pediment, and the corner akroteria were in the form of gilded bronze lebetes (cauldrons on tripod stands). The long sides were decorated by marble lion-head spouts, adapted to the sima of the roof.

The Olympic victors were crowned in front of the entrance to the pronaos, in a small rectangular space with a flooring of hexagonal marble slabs. Beside the SW corner of the temple grew the

Plan of the temple of Zeus. The main entrance at the east was approached by a ramp. The chryselephantine statue of Zeus, one of the seven wonders of the ancient world, was placed at the end of the cella, which was divided into three aisles by two rows of two-tiered columns.

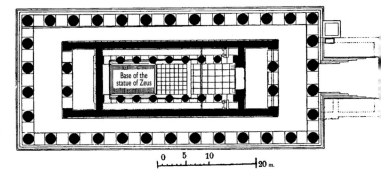

Base of the
statue of Zeus

0   5   10   20 m.

"beautiful-crowned olive", planted, according to tradition, by Herakles himself and from which the branch was cut for the victor's crown. Catastrophe struck the temple in A.D. 426, when it was set fire by edict of Theodosius II. Later on, in A.D. 522 and again in 551, it was further destroyed by two great earthquakes. The temple is a monumental landmark in Greek art, both for its architecture and for its magnificent pedimental compositions.

Restoration of the NW column of the temple was completed in the summer of 2004. This is the most important work of restoration that has been carried out in the Altis to date.

Standing *in situ* near the SE corner of the temple of Zeus is the high (some 9 m.) triangular base that held the **Nike** of the sculptor Paionios of Mende, now exhibited in the Museum. The dedicatory inscription and signature of the artist is carved on the third course of the base (a copy on the base, the original in the A.M.O.).

The **Bouleuterion,** south of the temple of Zeus, was the seat of the Boule (Council) of the Eleians and the Hellanodikai, whose task it was to oversee the running of the Games. Here too were examined the objections and violations of the athletes and here the penalties were decided. Construction of the building began in the 6th century and was completed in the 4th century B.C. Small

Restoration drawing of the temple of Zeus. To the right is shown the great conical altar of Zeus and, to the left, the base with the Nike of Paionios (F. Adler, Olympia II).

The temple of Zeus. The south colonnade, its columns toppled by earthquake, provide evidence for the cause of the destruction of the great temple.

Conglomerate stone was the material used for building the monuments of the Altis. This is a stone that is native to and plentiful in the region. Illustrated here is a detail showing the shell inclusions.

additions were made in Roman times. The Bouleuterion consists of two long narrow apsidal buildings, with a square construction between them, which was probably unroofed. An Ionic stoa was erected east of the complex in the 4th century B.C. The apsidal buildings, a distant echo of the much earlier prehistoric constructions, are divided into two aisles by a series of 7 columns. Perhaps the records of the Sanctuary were kept in the two small rooms formed in the semi-circle of the apse. In the square room stood the statue and altar of Zeus Horkeios, Here, before the Games, athletes and judges, standing on the genitals of a goat, took the sacred oath, that they would respect the rules of the Games and compete honourably.

South of the Bouleuterion is the **South Stoa.** It was built around 350 B.C. and it was the main entrance to the Altis. It has an outer colonnade of 34 Doric columns and an interior colonnade in the Corinthian order. This is the first monument at Olympia in which the Corinthian order was used. A monumental propylon on the south façade gives the building a T-shaped plan. The west part of the building has yet to be explored.

The area NW of the South Stoa is occupied by bathing installations, a Roman complex called the **South Baths.** Preserved among the remains is a section of the fortification wall that was

The Bouleuterion, seat of
the Boule of the Eleians
and the Hellanodikai.
One of the earliest of the
buildings in the Altis.
View from the southwest.

The South Stoa formed
the south boundary of the
Sanctuary facing the
Alpheios river. Shown here
is the interior Corinthian
colonnade of the Stoa.

The Leonidaion, a large hostel, occupies the southwestern part of the Altis. It was established in 330 B.C. by Leonidas the Naxian. General view of the building from the NE. Visible in the background are the baths of the Leonidaion and the southwest building (athletic club).

built when the sanctuary was threatened by the Herulians.

The visitor coming from the SW gate of the Altis again follows the Sacred Way, and at its western end, outside the sacred peribolos, he comes to the **Leonidaion.** This was a large hostel for distinguished visitors, built around 330 B.C. It is named for the donor and architect, Leonidas of Naxos, as given in the dedicatory inscription on the architrave of the monument. It is a large, almost square building (80,18 x 73,51 m.) with an Ionic exterior colonnade of 138 columns. In the center is a peristyle court with 44 Doric columns.

In Roman times, a decorative pool occupied the centre of the inner court of the Leonidaion

On all four sides there are rooms between the two colonnades. A decorative pool occupied the central court in Roman times, when the building served as a house for Roman officers.

Another hostel was erected SW of the Leonidaion in the 3rd century A.C., of which only a small bathing establishment remains. Because of its location it is known as the **Leonidaion Baths**. It comprises four small vaulted rooms. Still preserved are the mosaic floors, the sophisticated heating system in the walls and the excellent water-supply system of the building. A winery (press) and

The Baths of the Leonidaion are among the best preserved buildings in the Altis. These were the baths belonging to the destroyed hostel mentioned above. View of the Baths from the southeast.

b. Mosaic floor from the Baths of the Kladeos. The baths were built over the open-air pool of the earlier Greek Baths. The rooms were richly decorated with mosaic floors.

The Workshop of Pheidias was built with the same dimensions as the cella of the temple of Zeus. Preserved are the wall orthostates. The superstructure belongs to the Early Christian Basilica. View of the building from the SW. The Kronion hill rises in the background.

a glass workshop occupied the site in the 5th to 6th centuries A.C. This is the only building at Olympia with almost the entire upper storey preserved.

In the SW corner of the Sanctuary is the so-called **Southwest Building,** erected in the Ist century A.C. It was the seat of an athletic organization and it was probably dedicated to the hero Herakles. Its construction began in the reign of Nero and continued to the time of Domitian (A.D. 84). In the north part is a pool surrounded by a large open-air peristyle or colonnade. Behind this are three large halls and smaller supplementary rooms (kitchen, W.C. etc.). The niches in the north façade held statues in antiquity. The big central hall had a hypocaust system of heating beneath the floor. Excavation of the building was completed at the end of the 1990s, bringing to light a bronze plaque inscribed with the names of athletes, dating from the Ist to the 4th centuries A.C. It is displayed in the M.H.O.A.

To meet the constantly increasing needs of visitors, in Roman times hostels were added in the west side of the Sanctuary. The building complex comprises two large houses. The first, to the west, was built around 170 B.C.; the second was erected shortly afterwards. The plan of the buildings follows the fashion of the time, with rooms around a central peristyle court. The fine mosaics that once decorated the floors have not survived.

The first **Baths** for the athletes were built in the 5th century B.C. beside the river Kladeos. At the end of the 4th century B.C., the installations were extended westward. The 1st century B.C. saw the last significant enlargement with the building of a large hall at the south, which was equipped with a hypocaust. Contemporary with the first phase of the Baths (5th century B.C.) was the above-mentioned **pool** (24 x 16 m., depth 1.60 m.), the earliest known in Greek lands. Built over its south part in Roman times were the **Baths of the Kladeos**, much of which was carried away by the river, leaving little or nothing to be seen today.

The interior of the three-aisled Early Christian Basilica.

The Baths of the Kladeos occupied an area of some 400 sq. m. and comprised many rooms and spaces, such as an atrium, hot and cold baths, dressing rooms, steam rooms, bath-tubs, toilets, and even a small individual bath. The river Kladeos has washed away the west side of the complex. The walls were faced with multi-coloured marble and the beautiful mosaic compositions of the floors are still preserved. The building was luxurious, with many ample rooms, richly decorated in the spirit of the times. These Baths indeed were for relaxation and special luxury. They did not simply serve the needs of everyday, as did the Greek baths.

East of the Baths is the **Heroön**, dated in the second half of the 5th century B.C., a small rectangular building with a circular construction inside. Initially it served as a steam room for the neighbouring Baths. In Hellenistic and Roman times, it appears to have served as a Heroön since there is a small altar of ashes and clay bearing the inscription "ἥρωος" (of the hero) framed by an olive branch and found inside the circular construction. To which hero it was dedicated is unknown.

Built in the second half of the 5th century in the western part of the Altis, exactly opposite the Temple of Zeus, was the **Workshop of Pheidias.** Here the great Athenian sculptor made the colossal chryselephantine statue of Zeus, one of the seven wonders of the ancient world. The measurements of the building agree precisely with those of the cella of the temple (L. 32,18 m. and W. 14,50 m.) and the interior is divided into three aisles by two rows of columns. While it was being built, the statue was placed in the wider, central aisle. The gold and ivory were worked in the rooms of the main Workshop, which occupied the space south of and along the side of the large building. Many objects were recovered from these rooms and they are now on display in the Archaeological Museum.

The Heroon. General view from the W. The ruins of the Theokoleon are visible in the background.

Over the ruins of the Workshop, a three-aisled **Christian Basilica** was built between A.D. 435 and A.D. 451. The apse of the Church was at the east end, where once had been the entrance to the Workshop. The marble screen is still preserved *in situ*. The entrance to the Church is in the south side of the narthex, the floor of which was paved with marble slabs. Inscriptions are preserved in the narthex telling us about the paving of the floor and giving information about the various trades of the period. The wooden-roofed Basilica of Olympia, the oldest known Early Christian church of Elis, was destroyed in the earthquake of A.D. 551. Of the Workshop, only the orthostates of the walls remain. Both the superstructure and interior of the building belong to the church.

Between the Workshop of Pheidias and the Palaistra lie the ruins of the **Theokoleion** or Theekoleon, the residence of the Theekoleoi, the priests of the Altis and their helpers (who collected wood for the sacrifices), the explainers or guides for the pilgrims who visited the Altis, diviners and others. It was built in the 5th century B.C. and comprised initially eight rooms and a central open court. In Roman times, a similar but larger complex with atrium and rooms was added to the east of the original building.

In the western part of the Sanctuary, north of the Theokoleion, are the athletic installations, the Palaistra and the Gymnasium. The **Palaistra**, dated in the 3rd century B.C., is a large square building

(66,35 x 66,75 m) with a central court with Doric peristyle, enclosed by stoas with many rooms around them, such as the *elaiothesion* (room where the athletes oiled their bodies before exercising), the *konisterion* (where they powdered themselves), dressing rooms, baths, lecture halls for teaching by rhetoricians and philosophers, etc. The central court was where the athletes practiced wrestling, boxing, the pankration and jumping. The columns of the south side of the building and the columns at the entrance to each room were of the Ionic order. The Doric propylon at the NW corner served as the main entrance to the building and in the south side there were two subsidiary entrances. Thirty-two of the original 72 columns of the peristyle court have been restored. A little doorway at about the middle of the north wall provided communication between the Palaistra and the Gymnasium.

The visitor completes his tour of the site with a visit to the **Gymnasium**. The initial building was erected in the 2nd century B.C. A little later, in the 1st century B.C., a monumental amphiprostyle propylon of the Corinthian order was added at the SE corner. The Gymnasium comprised an enormous open-air court bordered by four Doric colonnades or stoas (120 x 220 m.). The athletes trained in the open-air court for the running races, the diskos throw and the javelin. The east stoa is the so-called "*xystos*", the covered colonnade equal to the Stadium in length (192,27 m.), where

West of the Altis, near the river Kladeos, there was a training area for the athletes. In Hellenistic times, a complex was built here comprising a Palaistra and a Gymnasium. View of the Palaistra from the SE.

The Palaistra. View from the NE.

the runners trained when the weather was inclement (rain or heat wave). To date, half of the Gymnasium has been explored. The west colonnade, where the athletes were lodged, is another victim of the river Kladeos and has been carried away in its torrent.

The east colonnade of the Gymnasium from the NE.

THE ARCHAEOLOGICAL MUSEUM

Anew Archaeological Museum to house the treasures of the Sanctuary of Olympia became inevitable with the earthquake damage suffered by the first Museum (the Old Museum) and with the accumulation of so many finds from the excavations in the Altis. Construction of the new Museum was completed in 1975 and in 1982 the exhibition of the finds was inaugurated. In the framework of renewing the exhibition for the Olympic Games of 2004 in Athens, the building was expanded and re-inaugurated and a new exhibition of antiquities was arranged in accordance with the demands of modern Museology.

The Museum building complex comprises the space devoted to the exhibition – antechamber and twelve galleries – with work rooms and auxiliary rooms in the east wing. The exhibition consists of incomparable works of art from the Altis. Through these the history, more than a millennium, of the most famous sanctuary of antiquity unfolds and the brilliant course of Greek art is displayed. True jewels of the Museum are the sculptures of the temple of Zeus, the Nike of Paionios, the Hermes of Praxiteles (the famous statue of Olympia). So too the cup of Pheidias, the helmet of Miltiades and all the bronze objects that are part of the richest collection in the world. The exhibits are displayed in chronological and thematic order, from Prehistoric down to early Christian times.

Clay jug with incised and impressed decoration. Early Helladic III period (K 1206).

Colonnade - antechamber

Displayed in the exterior colonnade of the Museum are architectural members from the buildings in the Sanctuary and statues. Among these is the impressive torso of a colossal statue of the Roman emperor Augustus, which stood in the Metroön.

In the antechamber, a model of the Archaeological Site provides the visitor with a full picture of the form of the Sanctuary in Antiquity.

Gallery 1

Here are exhibited the finds from the Prehistoric and Protohistoric periods at Olympia. The earliest evidence of habitation in the area consists of sherds found on the northern slope of the Stadium, that are dated at the end of the Neolithic period (4300-3100 B.C.).

The Early Helladic Period (3100-2000 B.C.) is represented by a wealth of pottery and stone tools that were found mainly in the area of the prehistoric mound (tumulus) of the Pelopion and in the

Incense burner of the late Early Helladic III period (K 14037).

Plan of the Archaeological Museum.

apsidal buildings, the earliest in the Altis (2500-2000 B.C.). In the museum cases to the left are Neolithic sherds, handmade pottery, anchor-shaped objects, tools, representative Early Helladic pottery such as sauceboats, jugs, amphoroid goblets, one-handled bowls, grayish coloured kantharoi, incense-burners, etc. Impressed and incised decoration beneath the rim, on the handle and on the base is found chiefly on jugs and one-handled bowls. This category of vessel suggests a connection with the Cetina culture of the Dalmation coast.

Pithos burials were found in the area of the apsidal buildings. From these came much pottery of the Early Helladic III-Middle Helladic I period, particularly askoi and kantharoi.

The Middle Helladic period (2000-1600 B.C.) likewise is represented by pottery and tools. Displayed are representative vases, such as askoi and kantharoi of a grey clay and a surface with a soapy-like texture, decorated with incised geometric patterns, and sherds of "Adriatic" ware. The stone tools are of interest: smoothed stones and points of pyrite and obsidian. Outside the Altis, prehistoric constructions have been found on the "hill of Oinomaos", one km. east of the Stadium, once thought to have been the site of ancient Pisa. Preserved in the foundations of the Museum is a large tumulus (2050 B.C.).

The Late Helladic or Mycenaean period (1600-1100 B.C.), which is divided into three phases, is represented by finds from the Mycenaean cemetery of chamber tombs found on the Zouni and Kalosaka hills around the Museum. The chamber tombs are the most usual type of tomb in Mycenaean times, especially so in Eleia. The typical Mycenaean pottery displayed here, with simple linear decoration, contained aromatic oil (stirrup jars) and ointments (rounded and cylindrical alabastra). There are also drinking vessels (kylikes), liquid containers (two-handled jars, amphorae) and so on. Other characteristic *kterismata* or grave goods are the clay figurines shaped like the letter *psi* (Ψ), a necklace of glass-paste and faience beads, weights (stone or clay loom weights, or dress decorations, as seen in the representations), objects for personal grooming (shaving blades), sealstones (superb miniature works of art for various purposes) and weapons (spearhead). They are dated in the Late Helladic IIIA -IIIC period (1400-1100 B.C.). The few Submycenaean finds (sherds and a kylix) bespeak the continuation of life at Olympia during this time (11th century B.C.).

The Prehistoric-Protohistoric unit is completed with the model of the prehistoric tumulus of the Pelopion. The collection shown in the gallery is complemented with the display of three large Late Hittite bronze sheets of Assyrian style (8th century B.C.) that were imported from the East and re-used as appliqué on wooden constructions or wooden statues. They have hammered decoration in zones showing a procession of priests leading animals to sacrifice, horsemen, men with scaly or laminated garments, etc.

Clay female figurine of Psi-type (Ψ), Mycenaean period (Π 2511).

Necklace of glass-paste and faience beads, Mycenaean period (Δ 28).

Bronze sheet with hammered representations. Late Hittite work of the 8th century B.C. (B 5048).

Bronze figurines of warriors (or perhaps Zeus), 8th century B.C. and first quarter of the 7th century B.C. (B 4600, B 2000).

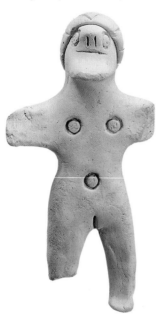

Clay female figurine with a diadem on its head, 3rd quarter of the 8th century B.C. (TC 2285). Probably represents Hera.

The earliest bronze tripod lebetes (B 1240), 9th century B.C.

Gallery 2

The uniqueness of the Olympia Museum in having the richest collection of bronzes in the world, is evident to the visitor to Gallery 2 where finds of the Geometric and Archaic periods (10th -6th centuries) are displayed. The **Geometric Period** (1050-700 B.C.) is represented by many finds, such as figurines of clay and bronze, miniature tripod lebetes (cauldron or basin on three legs), and metal sheets, displayed in the left side of the gallery. The large tripod lebetes, the most brilliant works of this time and the most characteristic dedications of the sanctuary, are on display in the right hand part of the gallery.

Hundreds of figurines were recovered from the thick layer of ash of the great Altar of Zeus in the Altis. The indicative number of the figurines displayed in the large case left of the entrance is connected mentally by the visitor with the hypothetical reproduction of the great altar in the background. Exhibited together with the figurines is the earliest monumental tripod lebes (9th century B.C.).

The Geometric figurines representing human beings are the earliest examples of small-scale sculpture and they come from local workshops of the Peloponnese (Argos, Corinth, Lakonia and Eleia). The human figure, in clay or bronze, is rendered in a strongly abstract style. It is schematized, with a rudimentary rendition of anatomical features, although the sex of the figure is emphasized. From these primitive minor works of art was born the human figure that later, after much searching and many trials, was brought to perfection by the archaic artist in the pedimental figures of the temple of Zeus.

In some of the earliest human figurines, archaeologists have recognised the great god of the Sanctuary, Zeus, and his wife, Hera. Some of the others represent warriors and charioteers. Some wear a helmet and represent, perhaps, Zeus Polemistes (Zeus the Warrior). The clay female figure wearing a diadem is likely to be one of the earliest representations of Hera (3rd quarter of the 8th century B.C.) and the bronze male figure with arms upraised may represent a god at the moment of his epiphany or appearance, if not a mortal votary. Another bronze figurine represents a goddess on horseback. Of particular interest is a bronze group representing 7 nude women in a circular ceremonial dance, a dance form that still exists in the Greek world of today.

In the third quarter of the 7th century, the human figure acquires volume and a profile. Characteristic of this time are the bronze figurines of warriors wearing a helmet and with one arm raised. They may have decorated lebes handles.

The clay and bronze animal figurines are very abstract and schematized. The horse and the bull are the most frequently represented. The colts are rendered with a narrow body, elongated muzzle and particularly long legs. The monumentally proportioned cast bronze horse marks the transition from the Geometric to the Archaic period.

The few Geometric bronze sheets decorated with simple geometric patterns and rosettes in dotted or hammered technique, were diadems or were applications (left hand case).

The bronze tripod lebetes, the most valuable dedications of the Sanctuary, were won as prizes in the Games as early as the time of Homer. They are displayed in the exhibition as representative examples of the Geometric period and fine examples of bronze working, with their variety in size. They range in size from the enormous to the miniature and they were found by the hundreds in the Altis.

a) Bronze figurine of a nude man or god wearing a petasos (traveller's hat), 1st half of the 9th century B.C. (B 1391) b) Bronze figurine of a nude man wearing a helmet (B 1698). Perhaps represents Zeus.

Bronze figurine of a god on horseback, 2nd quarter of the 8th century B.C. (B 1750)

Bronze figurines depicting a group of women in a circular dance (perhaps nymphs), 8th century B.C. (B 5401).

Bronze, solid cast statuette of a horse. The work marks the transition from the Geometric to the Archaic period. Early 7th century B.C. (B 1741).

Most preserve their cast legs, decorated richly with geometric patterns, such as spirals, circles, broken lines etc. (right hand case).

In the same case are shown lebes handles, the earliest of which are perforated and crowned especially with a little horse or colt. The later ones are supported by human figures. The two large bronze figures of the Telchinoi, mythical metal workers, were supports for this type of handle. This type of lebes was made from the third quarter of the 8th to the 7th century B.C. and it coincided with other types.

At the end of the 8th and beginning of the 7th century B.C., technicians came under the influence of the East. With the great wave of colonisation, Hellenism spread out along the coasts of the Mediterranean and the Pontus Euxinus (Black Sea). The colonists brought back works of art when returning home. The local artist was aware of these, and influenced by them. He imitated and assimilated them, while impressing his work with his own style and idiosyncracy, thus producing unique works of art that bound the influence of the East with the individuality of the Greek artist.

The art of the 7th century, known as "**Orientalizing**", threw off this influence as it developed and the Greek artist achieved greatness through the large-scale sculpture of Archaic and Classical times. The most representative works of the orientalizing style are the griffins, sirens and metal sheets. Late in the 8th century and dur-

Bronze lebes handle. Beginning of the 8th century B.C. (B 6341).

Bronze figurines from the decoration of a lebes handle. The left-hand figure perhaps depicts one of the Telchines, mythical metal workers, the right-hand figure a warrior. End of the 8th century B.C. (B 3390, 5700).

ing the 7th, a new type of lebes was in vogue that followed eastern prototypes. Applied around the rim of the vessel are lion heads, griffins and sirens. The base is conical with hammered decoration. The griffin protomes, datable in the 7th century B.C., are made likewise with the hammered technique or they are cast with inset eyes of bone. These mythical beings have an daemonic and apotropaic expression and they are exceptional examples of toreutic skill.

The sirens, mythical, daemonic winged creatures, which like the griffins were applied to lebetes, are dated from the 8th to the 7th century B.C.

A work that is characteristic of this time is the large lebes decorated with sirens, griffins and lions around the rim. Although the conical base on which it rests actually belongs to another lebes, it has been set here in order to give the visitor a more complete picture of the vessel.

Bronze griffin protomes (Br 8767, B 288). No. 8767 is the earliest hammered representation, 700 B.C. The other griffin is cast and had inset bone eyes that have not survived (7th century B.C.).

Bronze male winged figure that formed a lebes handle attachment. 2nd half of the 8th century B.C., eastern origin (B 4312).

Bronze winged female figure, a lebes handle attachment, from a Corinthian workshop of 670 B.C. (B 28).

Bronze winged female figure from a lebes handle attachment, 8th century B.C., eastern origin (B 27).

Large bronze lebes decorated around the rim with lion heads, griffins and sirens following eastern prototypes (670 B.C.).
The conical base decorated with scenes on hammered sheets (8th century B.C.) belongs to another lebes (B 4224)

Bronze lion head, imported from the east. Late Hittite work of the 8th century B.C. (B 4999).

Archaic period (7th/6th century B.C.)

The time of the great *floruit* of the Sanctuary, which was deluged with dedications, is represented by a wealth of bronze objects. These comprise mainly figurines and attachments of vessels, but there are also pieces of armour, such as shields, helmets (left part of the gallery), metal sheets, cuirasses, shield bands, greaves etc (right hand part of the gallery).

The daemonic, winged, female figure with the inset bone eyes (590-580 B.C.) in the centre of the gallery, is one of the rare large works in the hammered technique. One of her wings is missing and it is unknown if this was a protome or part of a statue. The bronze lion head behind her, imported from the East (8th century B.C.), might have decorated a building or else it was the protome in the center of a shield.

The hammered bronze sheets of Archaic times were applied as sheathing on wooden constructions, doors or door jambs and they come for the most part from Ionian workshops. Unique for both size

Hammered bronze sheet cut-out representing a griffin nursing its young. Product of a Corinthian workshop, 630-620 B.C. (B 104).

Hammered winged female daemonic figure, 590-580 B.C. (B 6500).

Bronze sheet with hammered decoration, perhaps for application to a larnax. Two centaurs trying to pound Kaineus, king of the Lapiths, into the ground by means of a tree. From an Ionian workshop (7th century). BElia.

Bronze sheet with hammered scene of a warrior bidding farewell to his family (perhaps Amphiaraos). The hero mounts his chariot while turning to say goodbye to this wife who holds their child on her shoulders and holds out her hand. From an orientalizing workshop of 580 B.C. (M 78).

and subject is the hammered bronze cut-out sheet in the form of a griffin nursing its young, the product of a Corinthian workshop. The eyes are of bone, inset. Beneath the belly of its mother, the little griffin can barely be detected. The holes around the edge show that the object was applied to something, but its use remains unknown. The remaining sheets are decorated with mythological scenes, such as the murder of the king of the Lapiths, Kaineus, by the Centaurs, the departure of a warrior, the murder of Klytaimnestra by Orestes, the abduction of Antiope, queen of the Amazons, by Theseus and others.

Other interesting examples of bronze working are seen in the accessories and fittings of various utensils. The utensils of this period had finely worked handles, supports and applications decorated with human figures, animals and other subjects. Outstanding among

Bronze sheet with hammered decoration in metopes. The first metope shows two heroes and a woman. In the second metope is shown the murder of Klytaimnestra by her son, Orestes. Elektra stands behind Orestes. At the right Aigisthos flees to safety at an altar. In the third metope Theseus abducts Antiope, queen of the Amazons. Product of an orientalizing workshop of 580 B.C. (M 77).

these are the products of a Lakonian workshop, such as the bronze statuette of a warrior, the figure of an old man with his staff (550 B.C.) and a bronze kore, probably the handle of a small lekane (basin) (early 5th century B.C.). The two confronting Sphinxes on either side of a floral decoration (570-560 B.C.), the reclining silens holding a drinking horn (530-520 B.C.) and the hammered bronze female mask with fine features (650-625 B.C.) that was applied to the face of a wooden statuette, bespeak the special artistic skill and sensitivity of their creator.

It is striking that such great numbers of weaponry and armour, such as helmets, greaves, shields, cuirasses, arrowheads, spearheads and spear ferrules etc should have been in the place where a sacred truce was held. Yet what else could be dedicated to Zeus Areios, who was worshipped as a warrior god, by the valiant warriors in thanks for the victory he gave them, other than their most valued possession, their panoply? Indeed, often enough the armour and

Bronze statuette of a warrior (B 5000).
Bronze statuette of an old man (perhaps Nestor, B 25). Both pieces decorated the rim of an open vessel. Products of a Lakonian workshop (550 B.C.)

Bronze handle attachment from a lebes in the form of two sphinxes on either side of a floral design. 570-560 B.C. (B 1710).

Bronze statuette of a Kore with girdle and slippers. It formed the handle of a lekane (χερνίβειον, hand basin). Early 5th century B.C. (B 3004).

Bronze statuette of a reclining silenos with a drinking horn (530-520 B.C.). With two other similar figures it decorated the rim of an open vessel (B 4232).

Incised bronze breast-plate, fully decorated (650-625 B.C.). Product of an Ionian-island workshop (M 394).

Hammered bronze mask from the sheathing of a wooden statue (650-625 B.C.). Product of a Lakonian workshop under Ionian influence (B 5099).

a) Inscribed bronze greave dedicated by the Kleonians. 2nd half of the 6th century B.C. (B 4465). b) Bronze greave. 1st half of the 6th century B.C. (M 907).

Bronze shield emblem with a hammered representation of a daemonic figure (2nd half of the 6th century B.C.). Depicted is a winged gorgon with lion forelegs and a fishtail (B 4990).

Hammered bronze sheet from a shield emblem (1st half of the 6th century B.C.). It depicts a winged gorgoneion (B 110).

weapons they dedicated were not those they had used in battle, but others, similar, larger or smaller and wonderfully wrought solely to be given to the warrior god.

The incised dedicatory cuirass, dated between 650 and 625 B.C., is a fine example of the skill of an Ionian workshop. The surface bears an incised decoration showing Zeus and Apollo with his cithara. Behind Zeus stand two gods and behind Apollo two female figures, Muses perhaps or the Hyperborean maidens. Animals and floral themes fill out the decoration.

Spiral patterns are used to render anatomical details on the bronze greaves. Some have a dedicatory inscription, such as seen on the best preserved inscribed greave in the collection. It was dedicated to the Olympian Zeus by the Kleonaioi (ΤΟΙ ΚΛΕΟΝΑΙΟΙ ΜΟΙ...Ν ΤΟΙ ΔΙΙ ΟΛΥΜΠΙΟΙ).

The shield exteriors were decorated by an apotropaic emblem. Among the most impressive is one with a hammered cut-out sheet showing a winged Gorgon with the legs of a lion and a fish tail.

a

b

Details are rendered by incision (2nd half of the 6th century B.C.). The hammered winged gorgoneion, from around the head of which spring three great wings to form a circle, is one of the most representative of the oversized shield emblems found in the Sanctuary of Olympia (first half of the 6th century B.C.).

Quite apart from the shield itself, the shield band (applied to the big interior handle) too, usually decorated with mythological themes, was often a special dedication in the Sanctuary.

Helmets, found in the Altis by the hundreds, are of three types. Most are "Corinthian", with a multitude of sub-types that give a full picture of their development from the 7th to the 6th century B.C. The "Illyrian" and the "Chalkidian" helmet is also represented. Notable among these is the Illyrian helmet the forehead of which is decorated with cut-out silver sheets (boar between two lions) and the cheek-pieces likewise (mounted horseman, 530 B.C.).

The defensive armour of the exhibition is completed with minor elements of the panoply, such as the forearm piece, the upper arm piece, the mitra (worn around the waist to protect lower abdomen

Bronze Corinthian helmets. a) Late type, end of the 6th-middle of the 5th century B.C. (B 5085). b) Developed type, middle of 7th century to beginning of sixth century B.C. (M 164). c) Early type, early 7th century B.C. (B 56).

c

a) Bronze Illyrian helmet deco-
rated with silver applications,
530 B.C. (B 5316).
b) Bronze Illyrian helmet, end of
7th-beginning of 6th century B.C
(B 5065). The Illyrian helmet is a
development of the Geometric
helmet. Its name comes from
the finding of the first example
of this type in the northern
Balkans.

Part of a bronze mitra with an
incised representation, from a
Cretan workshop (2nd half of
the 7th century B.C.). It may
depict Helen confronted by
Menelaos or Klytaimnestra with
Orestes (B 4900).

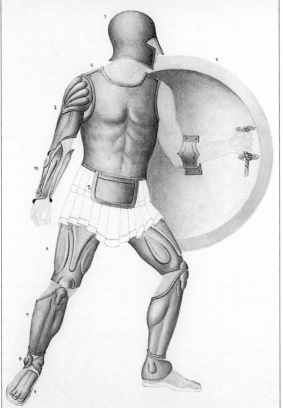

A representation of the panoply of an archaic hoplite. 1. helmet, 2. cuirass or breastplate, 3. upper arm guard, 4. shield, 5. mitra or loin guard, 6. thigh guard, 7. greaves, 8. ankle guard, 9. foot guard, 10. forearm guard.

Terracotta central akroterion of the Heraion. Archaic period (Π 2969).

Limestone Head of Hera or a Sphinx, 600 B.C. (Λ 1).

Terracotta head of a Sphinx (530-520 B.C.) from an akroterion of the Treasury of the Geloans (T 1).

and genitals), thigh guard, ankle guard and foot guard (see drawing).

Dominant in the gallery is the terracotta central akroterion of the Heraion (end of the 7th - beginning of the 6th century B.C.). It is unique in size and most of it is restoration. The little that remains of the original, however, preserves its original colour. The discoid shape, the relief surface, the combination of decorative themes and colours give the feeling of perpetual motion. Various theories have been proposed about the symbolism of the akroteria of this type. They are likely to have symbolized the sun or been an astral symbol.

Monumental sculpture of Archaic times is represented at Olympia by the colossal head of a goddess that was found in the area of the Heraion. It is likely to be Hera (it has also been interpreted as a sphinx), and it may have been part of a cultic group of Zeus and Hera that stood within the temple. The goddess with the characteristic smile of archaic art, the polos on her head and her large almond-shaped eyes, is the product of a Peloponnesian workshop of around 600 B.C.

Gallery 3

Displayed are pottery of Archaic and Classical times, bronze objects and fragments of architectural members belonging to buildings of this time.

The limestone lion in the centre of the gallery, one of the earliest works of monumental sculpture (680-670 B.C.), comes from a Corinthian workshop and served as the spout of a spring.

The pottery is, for the most part, local work or made in a Lakonian workshop. Typical shapes are the Eleian lekythoi and the Lakonian kylikes decorated with mythological scenes (cases on either side of the entrance). The terracotta female head of a Sphinx in the right hand case was an akroterion on the Treasury of the Geloans and it is a work of 530-520 B.C. from Magna Graeca,

Part of a stand, decorated with a palmette and confronting lions, 6th century B.C. (B 6100).

Worth noting especially are the bronze vessels and the attachments for vessels, such as the omphalos phialai (shallow bowls with omphalos in centre), the kadoi (situlae, case left of the entrance), lekanes (basins), tripod legs, lion legs, bases, beautifully worked handles (large left-hand case) and so on. These are brilliant examples of the toreutic art. Notable among them are the large cast tripod leg decorated with metopes, the base of an incense burner with a representation of a jumper, the floral handles and others decorated with human protomes or animals, the bronze statuette of a goddess with a flower, which was the base of a utensil, the bronze Sphinx and others.

Displayed in the same case is jewellery, such as pins and brooches, bracelets, bronze rings, and a vessel shaped like a frying pan, a ram's head from the rim of a lebes and others.

The terracotta architectural members are from the Treasuries. There are sections of terracotta cornices, their colours and patterns still beautifully preserved. The colours employed were brown, black, red, ochre and a whitish colour. The large corner piece from the painted terracotta decoration of a pediment belongs to the Treasury of the Geloans (right hand wall).

The north wall of the gallery is taken up by a section of the entablature and pediment of the Treasury of the Megarians, which is dated 520 B.C. The inscription ΜΕΓΑΡΕΩΝ (of the Megarians) on the architrave was added in Roman times. The scene in the pediment (L. 5,70 m., H. 0,75 m.) is the Gigantomachy, an especially popular theme in architectural sculpture. Of the II figures of the pediment, only the central one, which represents a giant, is still in relatively good condition. The others are poorly preserved. Taking part in the battle are Zeus, Athena, Herakles and Poseidon with Ares. Sea serpents and beasts in the corners of the pediment frame the gods and giants.

Palmette from the upper end of a tripod, late 6th-Ist half of the 5th century B.C. (B 5570).

Bronze lekane (basin) with ornate handle, of eastern origin, early 7th century B.C. (B 5758+Br. 1375).

Cast bronze tripod leg with representations in six metopes (600 B.C.). Product of a Corinthian workshop (B 7000).

Lion-footed bronze vessel, beginning of the 5th century B.C. (Br. 11554).

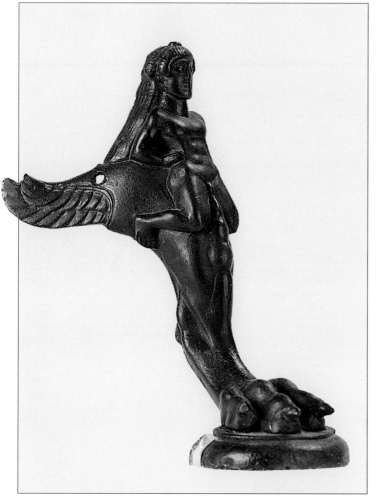

Bronze thymiaterion (incense burner) base in the form of a youthful jumper on a winged lion leg. Etruscan work of 480-460 B.C. (B 1001).

Bronze statuette of a goddess or kore holding a flower. It formed the base of a vessel. Product of a Peloponnesian workshop of 520 B.C. (B 5325).

Bronze Sphinx from the decoration of a vessel (late 6th century B.C.). Product of a Lakonian workshop (B 5300).

*Reconstruction of part of the entablature and pediment of the
Treasury of the Megarians, 520 B.C.*

*Corner of the painted terracotta facing of the pedimental cornices
of the Treasury of the Geloans, 2nd half of the 6th century B.C.*

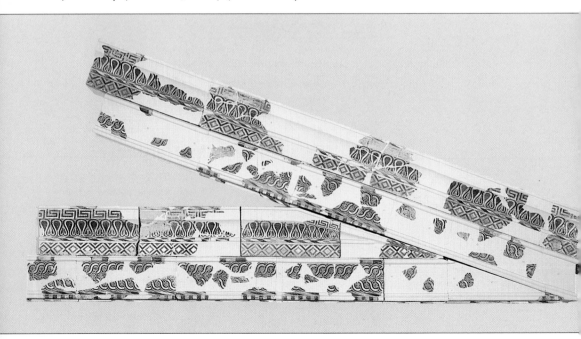

Gallery 4

Exhibited here are choice works of large-scale terracotta sculpture that were found in the Sanctuary. Pride of place is given to the terracotta group of Zeus and Ganymede. According to the myth, the father of the gods fell in love with the young prince of Troy, Ganymede and, transforming himself into an eagle, he flew down from Olympos to carry him off. The sculpture shows the moment when Zeus, having transformed himself back into human form, takes Ganymede by the hand and runs off toward Olympos. The god holds the traveller's staff and Ganymede a rooster, erotic symbol given him by the god. On Olympos, Ganymede became the cup-bearer of the gods and Zeus endowed him with perpetual youth. This splendid creation from a Corinthian workshop of 480-470 B.C., preserving still its colours in excellent condition, is likely to have been the akroterion of a Treasury. It is the first work of Greek art to show expression in the eyes, retaining still the slight smile left from Archaic times. The strongly triumphant expression of Zeus and the look of satisfaction on his face are in marked contrast to the serious and thoughtful face of Ganymede.

Clay dolphin leaping from the waves (400 B.C.). Probably from the akroterion of a treasury (TC 1093+4598).

Displayed in the case to the left of the entrance are fragments of a terracotta group of a Satyr and a Maenad (500 B.C.), perhaps the akroterion of a Treasury, as also the lovely clay dolphin leaping from the waves (400 B.C., right-hand case). The seated terracotta lion (middle of the 5th century B.C.) next to it has preserved its colours well.

One of the most characteristic examples of the severe style is the terracotta statue of Athena, part of a group from a Peloponnesian workshop (490 B.C.). The severe beauty of the goddess is proclaimed by the large almond-shaped eyes, the archaic smile and the curls that frame her face. On her head she wears an Attic helmet with crest.

The helmet of Miltiades (B 2600).

The over life-sized ear and horn belonged to a large bronze bull that was dedicated in the Sanctuary by the Eretrians after their victory over the Athenians around 500 B.C.

The terracotta warrior, product of a Peloponnesian workshop (480 B.C.), belonged to a group that depicted a battle.

Shown in the gallery are many bronze objects with the names of their dedicators. The Corinthian helmet and the Etruscan helmet that are inscribed alike, HIAPON Ο ΔΕΙΝΟΜΕΝΕΟΣ / ΚΑΙ ΤΟΙ ΣΥ-ΡΑΚΟΣΙΟΙ / ΤΟΙ ΔΙ ΤΥΡΡΑΝΟΝ ΑΠΟ ΚΥ[ΜΑΣ, were dedicated by Hieron, tyrant of Syracuse, and his compatriots after their victory over the Etruscans (*Tyrrhenoi*) at Kyme in Italy, in 474 B.C. A similar helmet with the same inscription is in the British Museum.

Bronze Assyrian (?) helmet (B 5100), the only booty preserved from the Persian Wars.

Terracotta group of Zeus and Ganymede, 480-470 B.C. (T 2).

Bronze helmets dedicated by Hieron, tyrant of the Syracusans (474 B.C.) (M 9 and 844).

Terracotta statue of a nude
warrior of 480 B.C. (T 3).

Bronze battering "ram", made in
a Sicilian workshop. 1st half of
the 5th century (B 2360).

Terracotta head of Athena, 490 B.C. (T 6). The goddess wears an Attic helmet and a diadem decorated with lotus flowers. Part of a group that may have formed the central akroterion of a building.

Cast bronze statuette of a horse from a four-horse chariot group, 470 B.C. (B 1000).

Bronze lekane handle with two lions felling a deer, ca. 480 B.C. Product perhaps of an Attic workshop (B 5110).

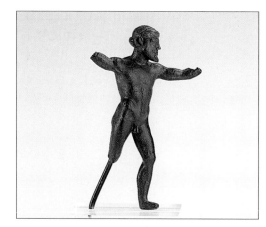

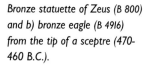

Bronze statuette of Zeus (B 800) and b) bronze eagle (B 4916) from the tip of a sceptre (470-460 B.C.).

The Corinthian helmet of the Athenian general Miltiades is of unique historical importance. Inscribed on the right cheek-piece is ΜΙΛΤΙΑΔΕΣ ΑΝΕ[Θ]ΕΚΕΝ [Τ]ΟΙ ΔΙ (Miltiades dedicated this to Zeus). That the helmet may have been the very one worn by the famous general in the critical battle of Marathon in 490 B.C., in which the Greeks won a famous victory over the Persians, makes a moving focal point for the exhibition. With it is shown an Assyrian helmet, the only booty remaining from the victorious battle of Marathon. Around the edge, the dotted letters of the inscription ΔΙΙ ΑΘΕ-ΝΑΙΟΙ ΜΕΔΟΝ ΛΑΒΟΝΤΕΣ tell us that it was dedicated by the Athenians as booty from the Persian wars.

The bronze battering ram is the only example of siege machinery preserved from antiquity; it is dated in the first half of the 5th century B.C. On each side it has the head of a ram in relief, and the bent teeth show that it had seen use before being offered to Zeus. The ram was attached to a long wooden beam.

The well preserved little bronze horse, rendered naturalistically, was part of the four-horse team of a chariot. It is the work of an Argive sculptor of 470 B.C.

The case to the right of the entrance contains inscribed bronze weights and utensil fittings. Notable among these are a handle with a decoration of two lions felling a deer (480 B.C.) and a beautifully wrought handle with a floral decoration and a winged female figure (430 B.C.). Dominant in the left-hand case are statuettes of Zeus with a thunderbolt in his hand (early 5th century B.C.), of Hermes (or perhaps a hunter or a shepherd, 480 B.C.), of the goatlike Pan (430 B.C.) and bronze figurines of an eagle, Zeus' symbol. Feet, curls and other parts of bronze statues bear witness to the numbers of dedications of this kind that once adorned the Altis, but unfortunately have not survived.

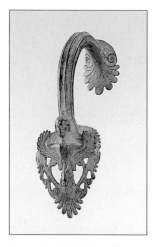

Bronze floral hydria handle with a female figure in relief, 430 B.C. (M 874).

Bronze statuette of Pan. The goat-legged god is shown as if dancing, ca. 450-430 B.C. (B 1601).

Bronze statuette of Hermes (?). Product of a Peloponnesian workshop of 480 B.C. (B 4310). The head gear and chlamys were added later.

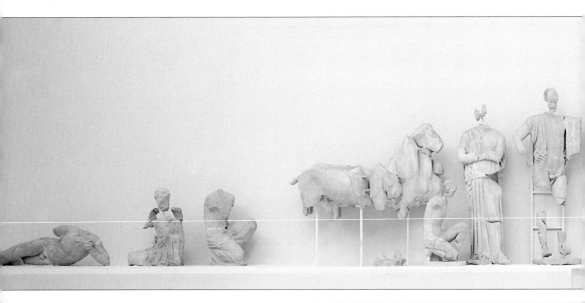

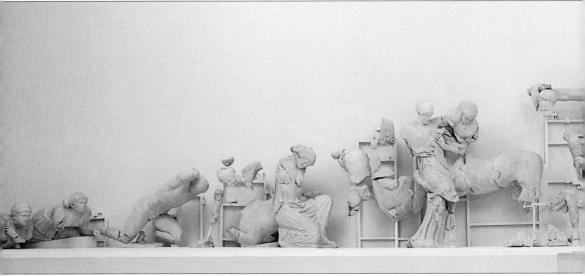

The east pediment of the temple of Zeus. Preparation for the chariot contest between Pelops and Oinomaos.

The west pediment of the temple of Zeus. Centauromachy.

Gallery 5

Democracy had been established in Athens by Kleisthenes at the beginning of the 5th century B.C. After the dramatic experience of the Persian Wars, Greece had drawn strength from her victories over the Persians, which determined the course of the Greek ethnos and indeed all of western civilisation. These violent events had an immediate effect on the social, political, religious and intellectual life of the Greeks, who now faced life in quite a different fashion. This was the time that saw the beginning of the most brilliant period of artistic creation. The immobility of the archaic figures disap-

pears to give place to harmonious and lively movement. The inevitable archaic smile is lost and the faces assume a serious, severe expression that suggests introversion and reflection. Indeed the early Classical period (480-450 B.C.), when these changes appear, is known in art as the "Severe Style" and it is the herald of the masterpieces of the Classical period.

Displayed in the central hall of the Olympia Museum are the most brilliant examples of the severe style of Greek art: the sculptured decoration of the temple of Zeus, which comprised two pedimental compositions with 42 figures, twelve metopes representing

East pediment.
Myrtilos or the groom.

East pediment. →
The river Alpheios.

East pediment.
The river Kladeos.

the Labours of Herakles, and lion-head spouts on the sima, all carved in Parian marble.

East pediment. A local myth, the chariot race between Oino-maos, king of Pisa, and Pelops, a Lydian prince, was chosen by the Eleians to decorate the east pediment of their temple. This is the only representation of the myth in large-scale sculpture. The composition s made up of 21 figures, which cover the surface of the triangular pedimental space (L. 26,39 m. and Max.H. 3,47 m.). The representation "narrates" the moment before the start of the terrible contest. In the centre stands Zeus, master of the Sanctuary and

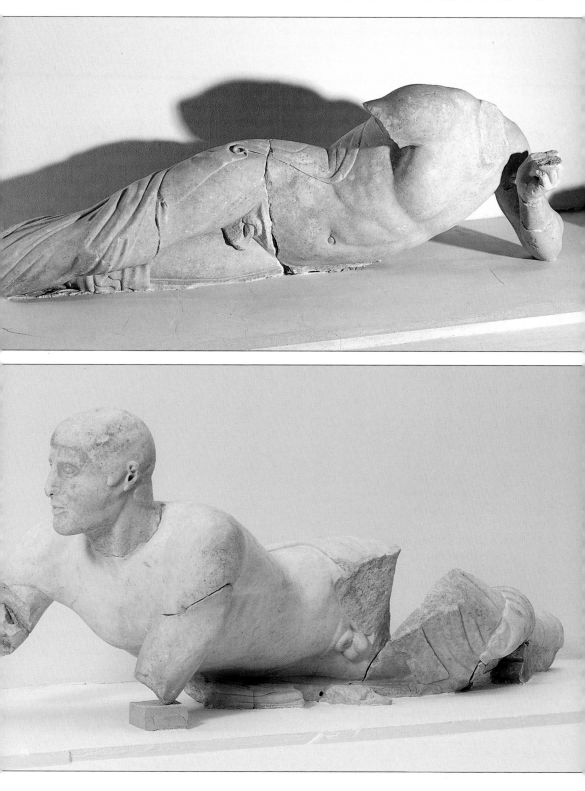

East pediment. The protagonists of the myth with their four-horse chariots.

invisible judge, holding in his right hand the thunderbolt. On each side of him are the main players of the myth, the couples Oinomaos with Sterope, and Pelops with Hippodameia. To the right of Zeus stands Oinomaos, helmeted and holding in his left hand a spear. Beside him, his wife Sterope has one arm bent across her waist, the other perhaps raised to her chin in a gesture of concern about the outcome of the chariot race. Before her kneels Myrtilos, son of Hermes and Oinomaos' charioteer, or, say others, groom. Following is the four-horse chariot of the king of Pisa, the four horses still partially preserved. Behind them the charioteer has taken his position in readiness for the start. Some scholars have interpreted this fiigure as Myrtilos. The next figure is a kneeling seer (Klytios or Amynthaon perhaps) and reclining indolently in the pedimental corner

lies Alpheios, the sacred river of Olympia. To the left of Zeus stands the young prince Pelops. His helmet is on his head and in his right hand he held his spear, in his left his shield. He is depicted nude with tautened body. Beside him stands Hippodameia, raising her Doric peplos with her left hand in the characteristic gesture of "revealing", known from wedding scenes. Her servant kneels before her. Then come the four horses of Pelops' team and behind that the astonishing figure of an old man who looks toward the centre and the protagonists of the tale. This is Iamos or Amynthaos or Klytios, the old seer of the Sanctuary. His expression is one of deep concentration, born of the gift of prophesy that allows him to know that victory this time will be won by the youth who came from afar and not by his king. His left hand rests upon his staff, while with his right

East pediment.
Youth playing with his toes.

he supports his head. With unusual skill the artist has rendered the old man's body and the anxious face with forehead creased. Next is the kneeling figure of a young man who fiddles with his toes and looks out upon the viewers. Reclining in the corner of the pediment is Kladeos, the other river of Olympia. The entire composition was emphasised by rich colours, no longer preserved, and complemented with the bronze arms and armour of the heroes and the bronze chariots drawn by the horses.

In terms of iconography, the pedimental composition is perhaps the most complete of ancient Greek art. All the players in the myth are there. The artist truly achieved a masterpiece, for he managed, with 21 figures, to depict in the best possible way the preparation for the contest of Pelops and Oinomaos, at the same time drawing the spectator into the myth in time and place. By showing the two sacred rivers in the corners of the pediment, he states that the contest takes place at Olympia, which lies between the rivers. By showing the charioteer behind the chariot of Oinomaos, he makes it known that soon the frightful contest will begin. The severe expressions of the faces and the stillness of the protagonists bespeak agony, worry and impatience for the dramatic outcome.

The positioning of the figures in the pediment has been the subject of many studies over the years and disagreements among scholars. For the present exhibition, their position in front of the temple and their measurements have been taken into account. Disagreement still remains as to the position, left or right of Zeus, of the two couples Oinomaos-Sterope and Pelops-Hippodameia, and about the identification of the two river gods.

The composition is masterful also from the standpoint of technique. The artist, assimilating what earlier centuries sought, has placed the figures in the pedimental triangles in unique fashion so that the

East pediment.
The old seer.

West pediment.
Apollo, framed by Peirithoos
and Theseus on either side and
by the groups of Lapiths and
Centaurs.

vertical and horizontal axes, formed by the standing, kneeling and reclining figures, predominate.

In the left corner of the gallery is exhibited a fragment of the inscription of the Lakedaimonians mentioning the golden shield they dedicated in the temple after their victory at Tanagra (457 B.C.) over the Athenians, the Argives and the Ionians.

West Pediment. From the phenomenal calm of the east pediment, the artist transports us with astonishing skill and control to the west pediment where another battle is shown at the height of its fury. This is the Centauromachy, the struggle between the Centaurs and the Lapiths. The myth tells us that Peirithoos, king of the Lapiths, who lived in the Pelion region, was celebrating his marriage

to Deidameia. Invited to the wedding feast were his half-brothers the Centaurs, who likewise lived in the mountains of Pelion. At the party, the drunken Centaurs broke the sacred rule of hospitality by trying to make off with the Lapiths' women. The Lapiths came to the rescue of their women, the result being the terrible fight that is spread out before us. Groups of Lapiths, Lapith women and Centaurs form an inimitable scene of battle, full of tension, emotion and force. The god Apollo (H. 3.10 m.) stands in the centre. In his capacity as god of harmony and order, with a single dynamic gesture of his hand, he tries to impose order. In his left hand he held a bow. On either side of him are Peirithoos and Theseus, the famous Athenian hero and friend of Peirithoos, who invited him to his wedding. Peirithoos is attacking the king of the Centaurs, Eury-

West pediment.
Group of Eurytion and Deidameia.

West pediment.
Apollo.

tion, who has seized the bride, Deidameia. The battle diminishes towards the ends of the pediment, where two reclining Lapith women observe the battle, their mouths half open through fear. Agony and tension is imprinted on their faces. Of the 4 reclining female figures, 3 are of Pentelic marble and were replaced in the 4th century (first to the left) and in the Ist century B.C. (the other two), when the originals were destroyed in an earthquake.

Among the groups, that of Eurytion and Deidameia stand out. The king of the centaurs has seized her by the hair, while she, twist-

Left wing of the west pediment. Lapith woman kneeling, from a group with a Centaur and Lapith woman.

Group of centaur and Lapith from the right wing of the west pediment.

ing her body, struggles to free herself from his amorous grip. The wild faces of the Centaurs with their brutal features, reminiscent of theatrical masks, are in complete contrast to the lovely faces of the men and women, especially those of Eurytion and Deidameia. Everywhere tension rules. In the faces, the movements, in the expressions of the people and in the horse-bodies of the Centaurs as well. It is all so vivid that you feel as if you see the blood raging through their veins, swollen from strain and tension. The result of this clash will be the victory of the Lapiths. "Here, in this pediment, you can see the full scale of the hierarchy: the god, man in his freedom, woman, the slave, the beast...The god stands in the middle, upright, calm, master of his strength. He sees the horror and he is not shaken –

The Lapith women in the left angle of the west pediment.

he subordinates anger and emotion, yet he is not disinterested – for he extends his hand to give victory to the one he likes. The Lapiths, the human beings, they too keep, as much as they can, the stamp of humanity on their faces immobile – they do not cry out, they are not overcome by panic – yet they are men, not gods, and a single light touch of the hand on the mouth and a crease in the forehead shows that they suffer. The women suffer even more – yet their pain, inexpressible, blends with dark shame....The Centaurs, the beasts, irrepressible in their erotic desire, drunken, loose themselves on the women and boys, they bite they howl, the logic to put order into brute force and civility into desire is missing... This is the extraordinary moment when all the ranks of life retain untouched their very being. In this moment frozen in marble all the elements exist together: godly firmness, the discipline of free mankind, the outburst of the beast, the realistic presence of the slave".

Who has better described the west pediment of the temple than N. Kazantzakis?

Stylistically, oblique and curving lines dominate the pedimental composition. They are formed by the sculptural groups and they frame the vertical central axes of Apollo, Peirithoos and Theseus.

Each of the myths of the pediments has a deeper meaning. For Oinomaos, after the hubris he displayed in killing the suitors, comes the cleansing. In the Centauromachy, the human spirit prevails against the wild forces of nature; the Greeks are victorious over the Barbarians.

Detail of the face of a young Lapith woman.

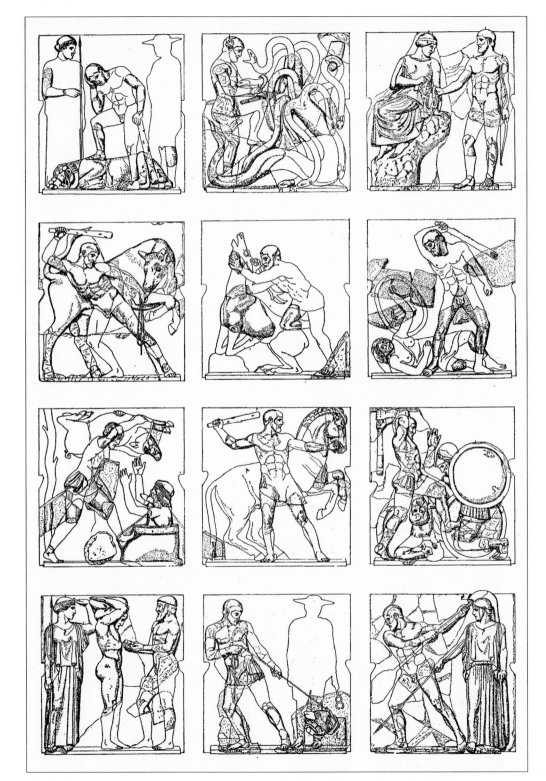

Metopes. Eurystheus, king of Tiryns, Mycenae and Argos, demanded that Herakles carry out 12 labours, in accordance with a Delphic prophesy, so that the hero would be purified of the murder of his wife and children, acts of the madness inflicted on him by Hera. The metopes illustrating the labours are above the entrance to the pronaos and opisthodomos of the temple, giving the beloved son of Zeus a prominent place in the sculptural decoration of the monument. Parts of the metopes (the lion in the first metope, Athena in the third, the bull in the fourth, the body of Geryon in the ninth and

The twelve metopes of the temple of Zeus. Reconstruction drawings.

The metope with the Lion of Nemea.

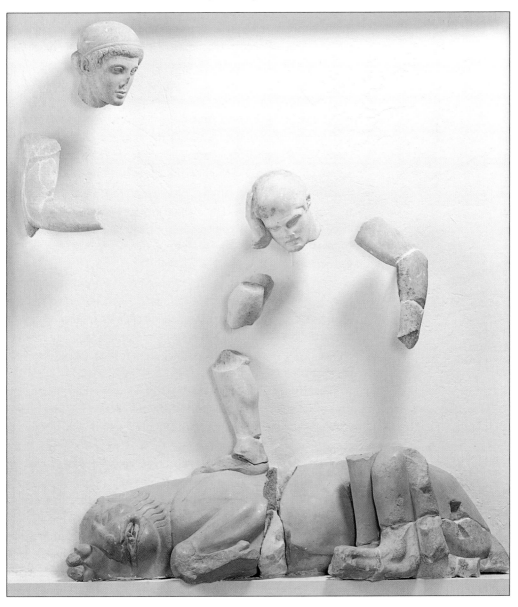

other smaller fragments), the visitor will see in copies, since the original pieces are in the Louvre Museum where they were taken in 1829 by the French mission of General Maison.

Above the entrance to the opisthodomos were the following metopes:

The Lion of Nemea. Herakles is shown in his first labour, young and beardless. Weary, he rests one foot on the dead lion, which had attacked animals and humans in Nemea. His helper is the goddess Athena. Of the original work, only her head has survived. Behind Herakles stands Hermes, with only part of his leg remaining. This is the first time that Herakles is shown as a hero exhausted from the struggle rather than at the moment of the frightful combat. The theme of the weary hero will predominate in the sculpture of the 4th century B.C.

The Lernaian Hydra. The snake-like monster with 9 heads, which lived in Lake Lerna, destroyed the crops and trees. Herakles finished him off with the help of his friend Iolaos. Preserved are the tentacles of the frightful monster, which the hero is beheading. Traces of colour still remain on the left part of the metope.

The Stymphalian Birds. The wild, carnivorous birds with iron wings and bills, lived in Lake Stymphalos, spreading terror. Herakles killed them with his arrows and gave them to his protectress, the goddess Athena. She sits, barefooted, on a rock, engaging like an ordinary little girl.

The Knossian Bull. In an extraordinary composition with the figures rendered in contrapuntal pose, Herakles captures the Knossian bull, which the gods had maddened so that it spread catastrophe everywhere. The metope is characterised by force and tension, tying it in with the forceful scenes of conflict in the west pediment.

The Kerynitian Hind. Fragmentarily preserved, the metope shows Herakles having caught the hind of Keryneia, the sacred deer of Artemis with the golden horns, that he was obliged to give to Eurystheus.

The Queen of the Amazons. The badly preserved metope depicts Herakles at the moment when he kills Hippolyte, queen of the Amazons, in order to take the beautifully wrought belt given her by her father, Ares.

On the other side of the gallery, the other six metopes, that were above the entrance to the pronaos, complete the heroic cycle of Herakles.

The Erymanthian Boar. The hero carries on his shoulder the

boar that had spread terror on Mt. Erymanthos in the Peloponnese. He is to give it to Eurystheus, who, in his terror, has found refuge in a pithos.

The metope with the Stymphalian Birds.

The Horses of Diomedes. Herakles has caught and bridled the man-eating horses of the Thracian king, Diomedes. The metope is reminiscent of the scenes in the west Pediment.

The Murder of Geryon. Geryon, a three-bodied giant who lived in the island of Erytheia, guarded the famous herd of cattle.

The metope with the Knossian Bull.

Herakles killed Geryon in order to bring the herd to Eurystheus. Depicted here is the scene of the giant's murder.

The Apples of the Hesperides. This is the best preserved of the metopes and the one that provided the total measurements for the others. According to the myth, Herakles was obliged to bring Eurystheus the golden apples, Gaia's wedding gift to Hera, which were guarded by the nymphs of the Hesperides. The apples were brought to Herakles by Atlas, father of the Hesperides, while the hero took the giant's place for a while and held up the heavens. In the metope Atlas has returned and is holding out the apples to Herakles. Athena, as a peaceful goddess, with an easy movement of her hand helps the hero who still supports the sky.

Herakles and Kerberos. Herakles pulls out of Hades its terrible guardian, the wild three-headed dog. Behind him Hermes can be seen.

The Cleaning of the Augeian Stables. The metope depicting the only one of the hero's labours that took place in Eleia, has been preserved in particularly good condition. Athena, this time as a warrior goddess with panoply, points out with her spear the place where Herakles is to dig so as to let in the waters of the river Peneios to flush out the stables. This is the first depiction of this labour in art.

From the standpoint of style, the metopes follow traditional archaic prototypes, for the Labours of Herakles belong to an iconographic cycle with long tradition. Yet they are also infused with the same pioneering spirit that is evident in the pediments. The metopes showing the Lernaian Hydra, the Erymanthian Boar, the Kerynitian Hind, the Amazon and Geryon are attached to archaic prototypes. In the others, the fresh and foreward-looking spirit of the ingenious artist is evident, and depending on the compositional axes, vertical, horizontal or oblique, they refer to the east (Nemean Lion, Stymphalian Birds, the Horses of Diomedes and the Apples of the Hesperides) or the west pediment (the Knossian Bull, Kerberos and the Augeian stables).

The lion-head spouts were especially impressive in their position around the marble roof. Artistically, they are in a class with the other sculptures of the temple. Since they were replaced from time to time if they were destroyed, they show an interesting typological development from Classical to Hellenistic times. At least nine different groups can be distinguished. Four lion-head spouts are on display.

The artist of the temple's sculptural masterpieces remains the great unknown. Pausanias tells us (V, 10, 8) that the creator of the east pediment was Paionios of Mende and that the west was by the Athenian Alkamenes. Yet scholars all believe that the traveller was mistaken, his information probably coming from "interpreters" of the Sanctuary. The stylistic characteristics of these two sculptors do not agree with the severe style of the figures of Olympia. Even today, despite endless discussion, researchers have not been able to reach a decision as to the creator of this masterpiece. Since various hands are

The metope with the Apples of the Hesperides.

discernible, the master artist appears to have had colleagues. The work is clearly that of a great master of ancient Greek sculpture who, with his forward-looking spirit was able to render the feelings of the heroes in the east pediment, within their very immobility and, in the west pediment, the victory of "Logic", the word, the power of logical thought, over "illogical", unthinking nature, in a dramatic encounter of mankind with the wild forces of the natural world. The sculptured decoration of the temple was finished in 457-456 B.C.

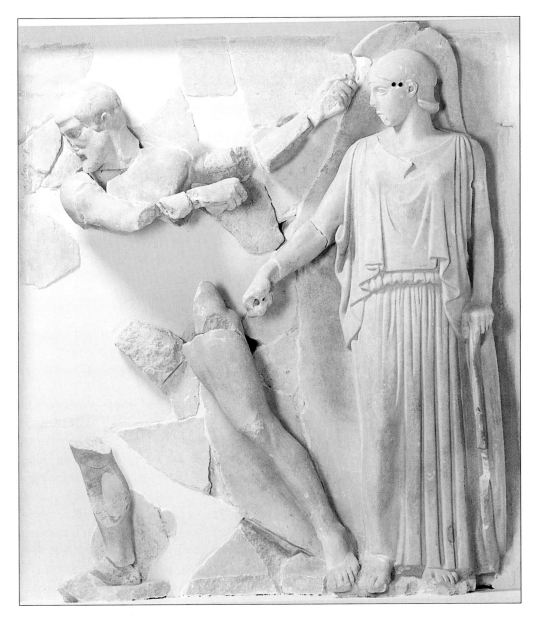

The metope with the Augeian Stables.

Gallery 6

The masterpiece of ancient Greek art, the statue of the winged Nike, by Paionios of Mende, stood on a high triangular base (H. 8,81 m.), still preserved *in situ* near the SE corner of the temple of Zeus. The Nike was 2,115 m. in height and the height of statue and base together was 10,92 m. The sculptor has rendered the youthful winged goddess in all her splendour, at the moment when she descends from sky to earth, setting foot upon an eagle, the symbol of Zeus. Her wings, and once-red himation, now destroyed, billow out behind and above her, giving thus a feeling of balance and of flight. The chiton of the goddess clings to her body, revealing all the details of her feminine form. The Nike is balanced on her right leg, with her foot slightly extended to rest on Zeus' eagle. Her face is not preserved because of the statue's fall. Missing too are parts of the wings, the body, her garment and the eagle's metal wings.

On one of the courses of the base is the inscription of the donors: ΜΕΣΣΑΝΙΟΙ ΚΑΙ ΝΑΥΠΑΚΤΙΟΙ ΑΝΕΘΕΝ ΔΙΙ ΟΛΥΜΠΙΩΙ ΔΕ-ΚΑΤΑΝ ΑΠΟ ΤΩΜ ΠΟΛΕΜΙΩΝ, that is, "the Messenians and the Naupaktians dedicated [this] to Zeus Olympios as a tenth of the spoils of war." Further down, in smaller letters, is the inscription: ΠΑΙΩ-ΝΙΟΣ ΕΠΟΙΗΣΕ ΜΕΝΔΑΙΟΣ ΚΑΙ Τ ΑΚΡΩΤΗΡΙΑ ΠΟΙΩΝ ΕΠΙ ΤΟΝ ΝΑΟΝ ΕΝΙΚΑ, "Paionios the Mendaian made this and the akroteria on the temple, having won the competition."

Thus we know why this unique work was dedicated. The Messenians and Naupaktians dedicated it to Zeus when they were victorious over the most powerful army of antiquity, that of the Lakedaimonians. The historical event to which the inscription refers is the battle of 421 B.C. in the last year of the Archidameian War. After victories in battle, one tenth of the spoils, known as the "tenth", was dedicated in the great sanctuaries. Inscribed statues preserved from antiquity are few, and the surviving inscriptions are of great importance for the information they contain. In the Nike inscription we have also the name of the sculptor, who is quite aware that he has created a fine work of art and he signs it. Significant too is the information that Paionios also made the akroteria of the temple of Zeus, having won the competition.

The Nike of Paionios is perhaps the most vivid statue of ancient Greek art. The great sculptor from Mende in the Chalkidike managed to harness an enormous block of marble, some 3 x 3 m., and create a winged figure of unique beauty, movement and liveliness, giving it a forward tilt so that it appears to have descended this very moment from the heavens. A small plaster copy of the dedication is on display in the Museum of the History of the Olympic Games of Antiquity.

The Nike of Olympia, a foremost example of the "rich style", is the first and most impressive of a series of Nikai that were made subsequently, such as the Nike of Timotheos in the temple of Asklepios at Epidauros and, two centuries later, the Nike of Samothrace.

The Nike of Paionios.

Gallery 7

After his work on the Acropolis of Athens, the great sculptor Pheidias worked at Olympia during the decade 440-430 B.C., where he created one of the seven wonders of the ancient world, the chryselephantine (gold and ivory) statue of Zeus. A workshop was erected in the west part of the Altis for the sculptor and his team. The colossal statue was set at the end of the central aisle of the temple of Zeus and there it remained until the end of the 4th century B.C., when it was transported to Constantinople. Written sources say that it was destroyed in a fire in A.D. 475.

The gallery is dedicated solely to the great Athenian sculptor. In the middle are a model of the Workshop and a large painted reproduction of the statue of the god. Information about its appearance is drawn from the few representations on coins and particularly from the valuable description of Pausanias.

The statue of Zeus was enthroned, and held in the left hand a sceptre, in the right a gilded Nike. The total height is estimated to have been some 12,40 m. It had a wooden core to which were applied gold sheets and ivory. The throne was constructed of gold, ebony, ivory, precious stones and inlaid glass decorative elements, and it bore painted pictures by the great painter Panainos. On its surface were mythological scenes in relief, such as the slaughter of Niobe's children by Apollo and Artemis, Nikai, Sphinxes, Charites, the Hours and so on. The nude parts of the god's body, the face, arms and hands, torso and legs were all of ivory, whereas the hair, beard, sceptre, the Nike and the himation were of gold. Glass flowers decorated the himation.

In the case left of the entrance, among the pottery from the area of the Workshop, a special place has been reserved for an extraordinary exhibit, a personal possession of the sculptor, known as the "cup of Pheidias". It is a little oinochoe (wine jug), inscribed on the base of which is ΦΕΙΔΙΟ ΕΙΜΙ (I belong to Pheidias).

Displayed in the other cases are moulds of various sizes, some of which were used for making the himation, other smaller ones for the glass decorations of the garment (palmettes, tendrils etc.). There are tools as well, such as the little goldsmith's hammer, bone spatulas, pieces of ivory, bone implements etc., that were used by the sculptor and his team for making the statue. Sections of the sima and antefixes from the Workshop complete the unit exhibited in this gallery.

Reproduction of the chryselephantine statue of Zeus.
Σχέδιο Κ. Ηλιάκη.

Bronze tools and fragments of lead decorative elements from the Workshop of Pheidias.

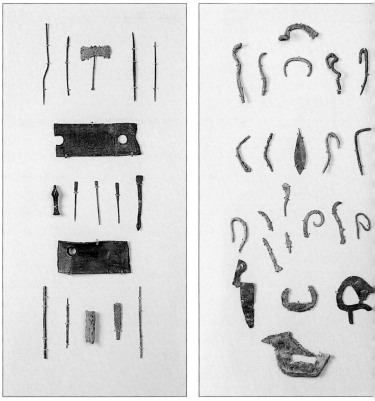

Clay mould for the folds of the himation of the statue, from the Workshop of Pheidias.

The base of the oinochoe of Pheidias (Π 3653), second half of the 5th century B.C.

Gallery 8

The Hermes of Praxiteles. The gallery is dedicated to one
of the foremost sculptures of ancient Greece, the Hermes of Praxiteles. The statue, 2,13 m. in height, made of Parian marble, was found
in 1877 in the cella of the Heraion, thus verifying the information
given by Pausanias (V, 17, 3) that in the Heraion stood a Hermes
holding the infant Dionysos, a "work of art by Praxiteles" (τέχνη δέ
εστι Πραξιτέλους). The god is shown nude, holding in his left arm,
which rests on a tree trunk, the little Dionysos, god of festivals, of
wine, of the theatre and celebrations. His himation has been thrown
over the tree trunk. His raised right hand held an object, now lost,
that he was showing to the child whose gaze is focussed there. It
may have been a bunch of grapes, symbol of the little god, as we see
in other groups of Hermes and Dionysos.

The left leg of the statue, missing from the knee down, has been
restored in plaster. So also the right shin and the lower part of the
tree trunk. In his left hand, Hermes probably held the *kerykeion*
(caduceus or herald's wand). Traces of a brownish red colour and
gilding are preserved on his hair and sandal. From the literary
sources Praxiteles is known to have collaborated in the colouring
of his works with Nikias, the great painter of his time.

According to the myth, Dionysos was the son of Zeus and
Semele. Hera, however, blind with jealousy, managed by trickery to
kill Semele before she completed the nine months for the birth of
Dionysos. Zeus then took the embryo and placed it in his thigh,
from which Dionysos was later born. So that the god who was
"nourished in a thigh and twice born" could grow up safely, far from
the wrath of Hera, Zeus entrusted him to the swift messenger of
the gods, Hermes, to take him to Semele's sisters, in Boiotian Nysa.
In the course of this long journey, Hermes stopped to take a rest.
It is this moment of relaxation that Praxiteles chose to immortal-
ize with his superb creation.

The statue originally stood some place in the Altis. In Roman
times, however, it was transferred inside the Heraion, where it was
set up in the cella in one of the niches on the right side. At that time
some work was done on the back of the statue, which led a number of scholars to think that it was a product of the Roman period.
Today, however, it is generally accepted that it is indeed a creation
of the great Praxiteles, and that it underwent some reworking during Roman times.

The Hermes is the perfect expression of the art of the 4th century B.C., a time when art was dominated by a strongly naturalistic

and realistic tendency, when the gods were shown not in action or participating in human activities, but quiet and in the relaxation of Olympian calm.

Gallery 9

Late Classical times - Hellenistic period (4th-1st centuries B.C.).
The Late Classical and Hellenistic periods are represented in the Museum by a few finds only, because the hundreds of statues of this time that once stood in the Altis have not survived.

Exhibited in the left part of the gallery are ceramics, figurines and two statues: the statue of a seated female figure (middle of the 1st century B.C.) and a small statue of a partially reclining man, perhaps Dionysos (late 4th - early 3rd century B.C.).

The right-hand case contains marble statue fragments and fragments of architectural members. Especially beautiful is the little head of Aphrodite of the Knidos type, thought by some to be a work of Praxiteles, by others to be late Hellenistic. The wall of the gallery is adorned with a sima from the Leonidaion and two Corinthian pilasters from the Philippeion.

Gallery 10

The Roman period at Olympia is represented by a great number of sculptures. In the gallery are statues from the Nymphaion, dedicated by Herodes Atticus and his wife Regilla, dated in the 2nd half of the 2nd century A.C. On the right-hand wall, in a semi-circular arrangement are the statues of the upper floor, representing members of the family of Herodes Atticus. They are in order as follows:

A portrait head of M. Appius Braduas, grandfather of Regilla, a headless statue of Regillos, the son of Herodes. A statue of Athenaïs, second daughter of Herodes, of the "Hereulanean" type, and another headless statue representing his father, Titus Claudius Atticus. In the central niche stands a statue of Zeus of the Dresden type, a fine copy in bronze of an original of 430 B.C. Next to it is a headless female figure of the type of the greater "Hereulanean", identified as Regilla, wife of Herodes, another headless male figure of a Roman wearing the tebenna, and with a scrinium (book or letter chest) by his left leg, identified as Appius Annius Gallus, father of Regilla. This is followed by the figure of Atila Kaukidia Tertulla, a member of the family, and the statue of Elpinike, the eldest daughter of Herodes.

A marble bull commands the centre of the gallery. It stood in the

←
The Hermes of Praxiteles, 330 B.C.

Red-figured "Eleian" bell-krater, 4th century B.C. The scene shows two maenads with a satyr between them (K 10243).

Marble head of Aphrodite, probably a work of Praxiteles (Λ 98).

*Marble statue of Zeus, of the
Dresden type, 2nd century A.C.
(Λ 108). Found in the central niche
of the upper level of the Nymphaion.*

Marble bull with the dedicatory inscription of Regilla (Λ 164).

Portrait of Lucius Verrus, 2nd century A.C. (Λ 166).

Page 113.

Marble statue of an himation clad figure. Some attribute it to Herodes Atticus (Λ 154).

Marble head of the emperor Hadrian (Λ 148).

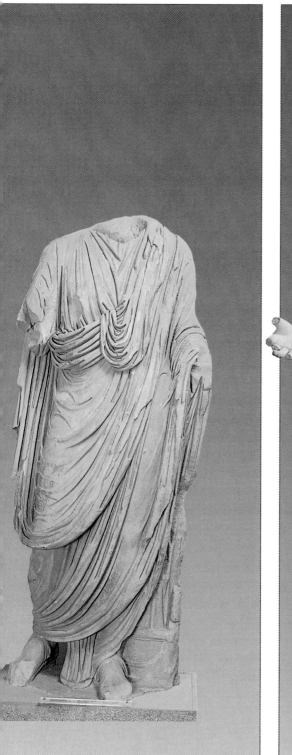

centre of the upper reservoir of the Nymphaion, as a symbol of the watery element. The inscription on one side tells us that the work was dedicated to Zeus by Regilla, wife of Herodes, who was in addition a priestess of Demeter Chamyne.

Exhibited in the left part of the gallery are sculptures from the lower level of the Nymphaion: a headless statue of Marcus Aurelius (161-180 A.C.), that comes from the monopteral (without a cella) shrine of the Nymphaion. The cuirass is decorated with griffins framing a lampstand and his shoes are of panther hide. Next is a female statue of Faustina the elder, wife of Antoninus Pius, and a statue of Faustina the younger, wife of Marcus Aurelius, followed by the small figure of a girl, pehaps Lucilla or Annia Faustina, daughters of Marcus Aurelius. Exhibited next is the head of a portrait statue of Lucius Verrus (161-169 A.C.) at an early age, wearing a diadem of laurel with a central medallion.

The Corinthian capital comes from the monopteral shrine of the Nymphaion. Next is a statue of Marcus Aurelius (161-180 A.C.). His cuirass is decorated with a gorgoneion, and beside his right foot is the trunk of a palm tree wth leaves and fruit. The statue of Hadrian (117-138 A.C.) represents the emperor as laurel crowned and clad as a general. Decorating his cuirass are two Nikai crowning a palladium, which is supported on the she-wolf nursing Romulus and Remus. Finally, the headless statue of the Roman *tebennophoros* from the monopteral shrine in the Nymphaion, is likely to have represented Herodes Atticus himself (101-177 A.C.). Next to the left foot is a scrinium with a key.

Gallery II

Displayed here are some of the statues that were found in the Metroön (left part of the gallery) and the Heraion (right part of the gallery). From the Metroön comes the statue of Agrippina the younger (15-59 A.C.), wife of Claudius and mother of Nero. The inscription on the base reads ΔΙΟΝΥΣΙΟΣ ΑΠΟΛΛΟΝΙΟΥ ΑΘΗΝΑΙΟΣ ΕΠΟΙΕΙ (Dionysios the Athenian, son of Apollonios, made it). That the empress is depicted as a priestess is evident from the himation being drawn over her head. Next is the portrait statue of the emperor Titus (79-81 A.C.), clad as a general and with an oak wreath on his head. The cuirass is decorated in relief with Nereids on hippocamps, dolphins and in the centre is a gorgoneion. His sword rests against a tree trunk at his right foot.

From the Heraion come the statue of an Eleian noble, a second one of Poppaea Sabina (first half of the 1st century A.C.), and a third representing Domitia, wife of the emperor Domitian (81-96 A.C.).

Marble statue of Agrippina (Λ 143).

Marble statue of Poppaea Sabina (Λ 144).

Clay figurine of a cat. A child's toy of the 3rd century A.C.

Clay doll or puppet in the form of a Roman soldier. It will have been a child's toy (1st to 3rd century A.C.) (Π 2218).

Glass vase from the Roman cemetery at Frankonesi.

Gallery 12

The exhibition in this last gallery is focussed on the final days of the history of the Sanctuary of Olympia. Here are utilitarian vessels, iron tools (hatchets, pick-axes, skewers, chains for scales, hoes, hammers, iron spits and so on), fragments of a terracotta sima with lion-head spouts, etc., from the Altis. Notable among the finds are iron seal-rings, lamps with scenes in relief and household utensils of clay.

Buried in the Roman cemetery of Frankonesi, 2 km. east of the Altis, were officials of the Sanctuary and athletes. The cemetery was in use from the 1st to the 4th century A.C. This is the source of the objects that follow: pottery, spindles and spools, dolls, figurines of animals, terracottas, bronze jewellery and other bronze objects. Of special interest are the very well preserved glass vessels made of translucent glass. Their typology is rich (saucers, perfume bottles, flasks and phialai or shallow bowls etc) and their chronology covers a long span from the 1st through the 4th centuries A.C. A single little trefoil oinochoe of blue glass alone belongs to the 5th century A.C.

The clay utilitarian pottery from the Altis, displayed in the next cases, demonstrate the continuation of life in the Sanctuary during the first Christian centuries. The epilogue of the exhibition is seen in the handmade pithoid vessels of grey clay, found during the construction of the Museum. They are the product of an establishment of short duration in the Kladeos valley by Slavic tribes during the 7th-8th centuries A.C.

Handmade clay vessel. (7ος-8ος αι. μ.Χ.).

*Reconstruction of the site of →
Olympia (Eva Mallwitz).*

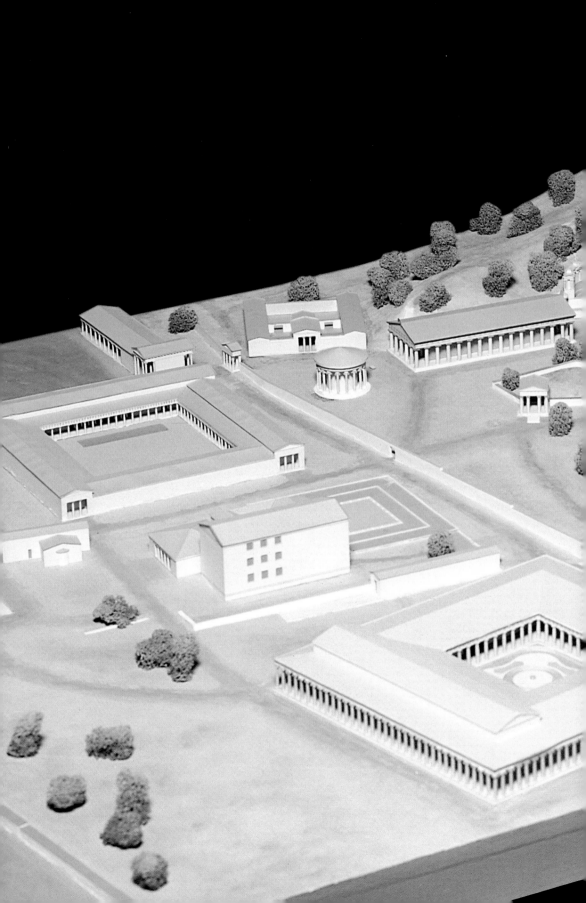

The Museum of the History of the Olympic Games of Antiquity (Old Museum).

Model of the Sanctuary of Zeus during its final phase.

THE MUSEUM OF THE HISTORY OF THE OLYMPIC GAMES OF ANTIQUITY

The exceedingly beautiful classical revival building that commands the little hill NW of the Sanctuary of Zeus is the Old Museum or Syngreion, designed by the German architects, W. Doerpfeld and F. Adler, whose names are connected with the first systematic excavations at Olympia. Its construction began after the first excavations in the Altis, with the national benefactor Andreas Syngros as donor, and it was finished in 1888. It is the oldest regional Museum in Greece and in the general Mediterranean basin. Until the decade of 1970, the Syngreion housed the brilliant finds of the Sanctuary, but the building itself had already been damaged in the earthquake that struck the area in 1954. With the construction of the New Archaeological Museum, the Old Museum remained closed until it was renovated from the foundations up. Since 2004, it has served as the Museum of the History of the Olympic Games of Antiquity.

The brilliant history of the Olympic Games, the most venerable institution of mankind, is presented through 463 exhibits that range in date from Prehistoric times to the 5th century A.C. They come from the Sanctuary of Zeus at Olympia and from other Museums of the region. They are presented in thematic groups, with a brief comment also on the other Panhellenic Games.

The Museum comprises an antechamber and a large central hall with ten smaller galleries around it. The thematic units making up the exhibition are: the prehistory of athletics - the beginning of the Games at Olympia (gallery 1), Zeus and his cult, the organisation of the Games (gallery 2), the preparation of the athletes (galleries 3 and 4), women and athletics (gallery 5), the programme of the Games-contests (central hall 6), the victors of the Games (gallery 7), prizes - dedications (gallery 8), the spectators of the Games, Hellenistic and Roman times (gallery 9), the Pythian Games (gallery 10), The Nemean -Isthmian Games and the Panathenaia (gallery 11).

On display in the antechamber are 4 models showing the chronological development of the Sanctuary, and busts of the two great researchers of Olympia, E. Curtius and W. Dörpfeld.

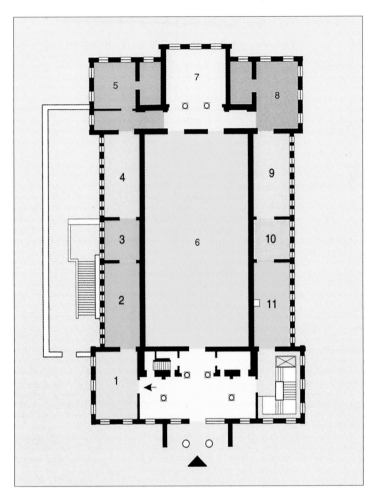

Ground plan of the Museum.

The history of the games

The Olympic Games were the most important panhellenic games in ancient Greece. Pindar sings of them in his first Olympic ode: "As water is the most valuable of the elements and as gold shines out as the most costly of all goods, and as the sun flares up more brightly than any other star, so shines Olympia casting all other games into the shade."

As early as Mycenaean times, games, of a local nature to be sure, were held at Olympia. From Pausanias we know that in 776 B.C., following an oracle, the games were reorganized by Iphitos and became panhellenic in character. They soon became the most important of the games, expressing the ideals of Greek athletics and culture. Athletics, an inherent part of Greek education, and the competitive spirit of the Greeks that was evident in all human activity, forged the Olympic ideals: noble rivalry, the conception of the "*kalos k'agathos*" (virtuous and noble) citizen. For whole centuries the best of the athletes from all over the Greek world gathered at Olympia for the Games, following the rules of noble rivalry, of competing rather than contending against each other, and to honour Zeus, the supreme divinity.

In Archaic and Classical times, the Games reached the height of their glory.

By Hellenistic times their purely religious character was lost and they became professional athletic exhibitions. Indicative of the loss of the original idealism of the institution were the punishments imposed for the first time in the 4th century (388 B.C.).

In Roman times the decline of the Games began, yet they continued for centuries in a new form, being ended in A.D. 393 by the emperor of Byzantium, Theodosios I. Until that time, there had been 293 Olympiads.

The institution was revived after 15 centuries, thanks to the efforts of Pierre de Coubertin and others, among whom Demetrios Vikelas was an enthusiastic supporter, and the first Olympic Games of modern times were held in Athens in 1896.

Bull-jumping was the most spectacular of the Cretan athletic activities. The jumper seized the bull by the horns while it was running and then made a dangerous leap over its back, to land on the ground. Bull-leaping was a purely religious ceremony (bull-leaping scene from Knossos, Herakleion Museum).

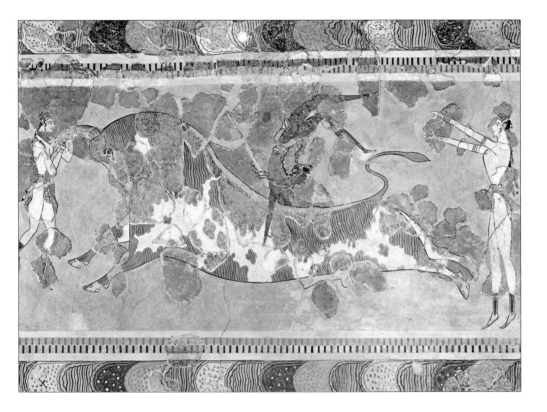

Gallery I

A. The Prehistory of athletics.

The first varieties of athletics in the Greek world go back to the beginning of the second millennium B.C. in Crete when a number of athletic activities appear in connection with religious ceremonies. The favourites were pole-vaulting, wrestling, boxing and bull-jumping.

The Mycenaeans in their turn inherited these games from the Minoans, introducing also new sports such as chariot racing and running. They were the creators of the competitive spirit and athletics became a basic part of Mycenaean life. They dedicated their "*athla*" (athletic contests), their funerary games in honour of fallen heroes, such as when Achilles organized the "games for Patroklos" in honour of his dead friend (Iliad, XXIII, 262 ff.). The contests described by Homer in the "games for Patroklos" are: chariot racing, boxing, wrestling, running, armed combat, diskos throwing, archery and javelin throwing. Described in the Odyssey are the games organized by Alkinoos, king of the Phaiakians, with specialized athletes, to honour his guest Odysseus.

The Prehistory of the games is presented through finds of the Minoan and Mycenaean civilisations. Displayed in the left-hand wall-case are excellent examples of the art of the sealstone, with the earliest representations of athletic games. Notable among these are two gold seal-rings that show the extraordinary skill of the Mycenaean artist. One, from Antheia Kalamata, has an oval bezel with a bull-jumping scene, and the other, from Achaia, shows two runners.

Notable among the Mycenaean pottery that comes next in the display, is a large Mycenaean krater (from Voudeni in Achaia, 12th century B.C.), with a figure in a chariot that suggests funerary games. Such contests are suggested also by the bull-shaped rhyton from Crete with a scene of bull-jumping (early 2nd millennium B.C.),

Gold seal-ring with a bull-leaping scene (14th-13th century B.C.), from Hellenika Antheias (Kalamata, Benakeion Museum AE 4048).

Gold seal-ring with a representation of runners, from the Mycenaean cemetery at Porta Achaias (LH IIIA, Patras, Archaeological Museum AE 4729).

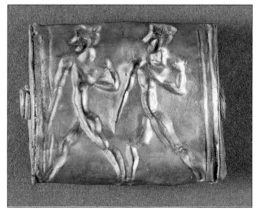

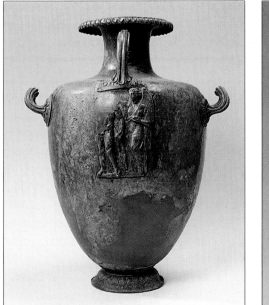

and by a chariot model from the cemetery of Prosymne in the Argolid (14th-13th centuries B.C.).

B. The beginning of the games. Tradition has it that the gods were the first to compete at Olympia. Zeus was victorious against Kronos in a wrestling match, Apollo won over Hermes in a footrace and he beat Ares in boxing. The ancient sources mention also many heroes as founders of the Games.

To Mycenaean tradition belongs the myth of Pelops who, after defeating Oinomaos, organized chariot races as funerary games in honour of the dead Pisan king and as a celebration in thanks to the gods for his victory.

According to other myths, the founder of the Games was the demi-god Herakles, who was the first to organize foot races and chariot races. He is the one who brought the wild olive from the land of the Hyperboreans, planted it in the Sanctuary and set out the boundaries of the Altis.

Pausanias names as founder of the Games the Idaian Herakles with his four brothers, the Daktyls or Kouretes, who came to Olympia from Crete. This Herakles first organized running contests for his brothers, determined the length of the Stadium and crowned the victor with wild olive.

Also mentioned among the founders are Neleus, Pelias and Pisos, the eponymous hero of Pisatis.

Bronze hydria with a representation of Herakles - Nike, from Elis. 3rd century B.C. (Olympia, Archaeological Museum M 2791).

Marble torso of Herakles, the founder of the Games, 3rd century B.C. (Naupaktos, Archaeological Collection ΣΝ 73).

Bronze tripod leg with a representation of the battle of Herakles and Apollo for possession of the Delphic Tripod. The second metope shows two confronting lions on either side of the tree of life, 8th century B.C. (Olympia, Archaeological Museum B 1730).

Strabo believed that the Games were established by Oxylos, the king of the Heraklids, after their descent (IIth century B.C.). The Games were later reorganized (776 B.C.) by Iphitos, who agreed on a sacred truce with Lykourgos, the king of Sparta, and Kleosthenes, the king of Pisa.

The written sources refer to 776 B.C. as the year of the beginning of the Games. The list of Olympic victors refers back to that year, but it was compiled much later. In fact, the first reorganized Olympic Games occurred in 776 B.C. This unit of the exhibition comprises objects connected with the mythical founder of the Games, the demi-god Herakles: black-figured pottery (lekythoi, skyphoi, amphorae etc.) of the 5th century B.C. showing the deeds of the hero, a small fragment of the upper torso of a statuette of Herakles (510-500 B.C.) from the Acropolis, a bronze tripod leg from the Altis with one of the earliest mythological scenes, the contest of Herakles and Apollo for the Delphic tripod, a bronze hydria with a representation of Herakles and Nike in relief below the handle, and the torso of a marble statue of the hero.

Gallery 2

A. Zeus and his cult. The worship of Zeus at Olympia was established during the Geometric period, as indicated by the numerous dedications, especially tripod cauldrons (lebes, lebetes) and figurines of humans and animals, examples of which are shown here. The clay and bronze figurines of little horses, the figurines of charioteers and the clay chariot wheels, refer to the first equestrian and chariot races that took place in Olympia at that time. Of special interest among the pieces exhibited in this unit are the cast bronze tripod legs, lebes (cauldron) handles, little bronze horses, bronze charioteer figurines (8th century B.C.), clay chariots with their charioteers, a bronze statuette of Zeus, a Lakonian kylix showing Zeus and Hera and a bronze head of Zeus, a copy of a work on display in the National Archaeological Museum (left-hand case).

On display also are small bronze wheels and little horses, miniature tripod cauldrons from Olympia, geometric pottery with a representation of a chariot race, such as the Attic amphora (720-700 B.C.) and the Attic pyxis with horses on the lid (750-735 B.C.) from the Ancient Agora of Athens (right-hand case).

B. The organizing of the Games. The Pisans were the organizers of the games from 668 to 572 B.C. From 570 B.C. on, the organization was definitively in the hands of the Eleians, who had

Bronze figurines of charioteers, 9th-8th century B.C. (Olympia, Archaeological Museum B 1671, 1670).

Bronze statuette of Zeus, protector of Olympia, depicted holding his thunderbolt and ready to hurl it, 480 B.C. (Olympia, Archaeological Museum B 5778 + B 5500).

Bronze inscription recording rules for athletes and judges. Last quarter of the 6th century B.C. (Olympia, Archaeological Museum B 6075, 6116).

seized the kingdom of Pisa. The Olympic Games were held every full four years, that is, on every fifth year. The period between the Games was known as an Olympiad, a term that is also used for the Games themselves. They were held during the first full moon after the vernal equinox, the eighth month of the solar calendar (modern July-August). Until 684 B.C. (the 24th Olympiad), there were six contests and the Games were all held in the course of a day. As the number of contests increased (in Classical times the number had reached 18), so did the duration, which reached five days. The Olympiads formed the basic chronological system of the ancient Greeks.

All free Greek citizens had the right to participate in the Games, unless they had committed murder or sacrilege. Barbarians and slaves as well were excluded from participating. Later on, the Romans tried to prove that their origin was Greek in an effort to take part. Women were limited to ownership of horses and chariot teams, and could not otherwise participate.

The Games were open to all as spectators, even to Barbarians and slaves, but married women were excluded. This severe ruling that excluded married women from watching the Games remains unexplained. Only the priestess of the goddess Demeter Chamynes was present, seated on the altar of the goddess, on the north embankment of the Stadium. The punishment for any woman who broke the law of prohibition was to be cast from the heights of Typaios, a mountain south of the Sanctuary.

The officials responsible for seeing that the rules were kept (called the "canons of Zeus", or customs established by Zeus), were the Hellanodikai. Until 584 B.C., the institution was hereditary and the position was held for life. Later on, the citizens of Elis chose the Hellanodikai by lot. Their term of office was one Olympiad and for ten months they stayed in the Hellanodikaion in Elis, where they were taught the regulations of the Games. They were responsible for organizing and running the Games and for the awarding of the prizes. They had the power to impose punishment, both financial and physical, and they could bar athletes from participation. From the fines that were imposed, bronze statues of Zeus were made. These were known as "Zanes" and they stood in front of the entrance to the Stadium. The number of Hellanodikai steadily increased. Initially there were two, then nine, later on twelve, then eight, and from 348 B.C. to the end of the Games, there were ten. During the Games, they wore a red mantle and sat in the exedra in the south side of the Stadium.

The Games were proclaimed by libation-bearers (*spondophoroi*)

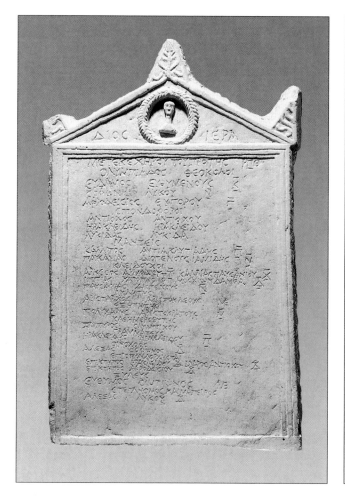

who were crowned with olive and bore the message of the sacred truce from city to city. The institution of the sacred truce was established in 776 B.C. by Iphitos. While it was in force, initially for a month, later on for three, all hostilities ceased and entrance to Eleia was forbidden to anyone bearing arms or to any army contingent, under threat of the death penalty. Breaking of the truce was punishable by exclusion from the Games. Interestingly enough, in all the 1169 years' duration of the Games, breaking of the truce was rare and minor. Clearly, the institution of the sacred truce, completely respected by all the ancient Greeks, was stronger and lasted longer than has any other peace agreement in the history of mankind.

The Games were of two sorts: gymnastic and equestrian. The gymnastic contests took place in the Stadium and the equestrian in the hippodrome.

Our information about their organization comes from the

Marble roof tile from the temple of Zeus inscribed with the names of the temple officials of the 189th Olympiad (28-24 B.C., Olympia, Archaeological Museum Λ 535).

Large bronze stele inscribed with a list of athletes, from the Athletic Club building of the Sanctuary. 1st century B.C.- 4th century A.C. Among the names is that of Athenaios Zopyros, who was an Olympic victor in the Pankration for youths in A.D.385. (Olympia, Archaeological Museum, Inv. 1148).

Representation of a Gymnasium. The athletes are exercising in the open central court. The young men completed their training in the Gymnasia. In addition to bodily exercise, the athletes listened to the orators, philosophers and politicians who frequented such places (drawing by K. Iliakis, Ekdotike Athenon archive).

ancient literary sources and also from the multitude of inscriptions that were found in the Sanctuary, some of which are displayed in this gallery.

An inscription on a marble roof tile of the temple of Zeus (28-24 B.C.) records the personnel of the Sanctuary during the 189th Olympiad. On a large stone, a fragmentary inscription records rules of the Games (1st-2nd century A.C.). The inscription on a stone statue base says that the statue was dedicated by Theoxena for her son Alkias, who was a *spondophoros* (right-hand wall).

Displayed in the left-hand case are bronze inscriptions from the Altis that record the names of the Hellanodikai, a list of athletes and rules of the Games.

Gallery 3

The preparation of the Athletes. The chosen athletes of the participating cities, who had trained under the guidance of the athletics trainer and the gymnastics instructor, came to Elis, the city in charge of organizing the Games, a month before they began. There they underwent preparation all together in the city's two Gymnasia

Marble base with figures in relief of athletes preparing for contests. End of the 4th century B.C. From the NW slope of the Acropolis (Athens, Acropolis Museum AE. 3176+5460).

and the Palaistra. In Elis too the Hellanodikai excluded those athletes who were not well prepared, so that only the flower of Greek athletics should contend in the Stadium of Olympia. There will have been trial games as well. Once at Olympia, training was carried out in the Gymnasium and the Palaistra. Before training, the oilers massaged the athletes' bodies with oil in order to loosen up their muscles. Then they put a powdery dust on their bodies so they would not slip during training. This preparation was carried out in special rooms of the Palaistra, called the *elaiothesion* (oiling room) and the *konisterion* (powdering room). After training, the athletes removed the oil, dust and sweat from their bodies with a strigil, and then had a bath.

The displays in Gallery 3 concern the preparation of the athletes. The marble base, from the NW slope of the Acropolis, is decorated in relief with a scene of athletes getting ready for the contest.

Gallery 4

The unit of the athletes' preparation continues in gallery 4. At the right wall are grave stelai with representations of athletes in relief, such as the athlete with strigil (*apoxyomenos* or athlete scraping

Marble relief showing an athlete scraping himself with a strigil to remove oil, dust and sweat from his body after exercising. 330-320 B.C. (Athens, National Archaeological Museum AE 888).

The aryballos was a small container for aromatic or ordinary oil that was used by athletes for oiling the body. Oiling and massaging before and after exercise was done by bath attendants. The process was a necessary part of the athlete's proper preparation (Corinth, Archaeological Museum T 3230, 29, 38).

himself, 330-320 B.C.), the athlete with strigil and aryballos (early 4th century B.C.) and the trainer-athlete (4th century B.C.).

Displayed in the left-hand case are black and red-figured pottery of the 6th - 4th centuries B.C., such as large bell-kraters, skyphoi, kylikes, etc., with scenes showing athletes preparing themselves in the Palaistras, and miniature aryballoi (7th-6th centuries B.C.

Of interest are the bronze strigils that were found in the Sanctuary of Olympia, some with dedicatory inscriptions, some with incised decorations.

Gallery 5

Women and athletics. Women could not take part in the Olympic Games except as owners of horses or chariot teams in the

Marble grave stele showing an athlete listening to the instructions of his teacher. From Glyphada, Attica, 400-350 B.C. (Piraeus, Archaeological Museum AE 3742).

Red-figured bell-krater from Olynthos showing athletes preparing for exercise or contest, 360 B.C. (Thessalonike, Archaeological Museum AE 874).

equestrian races, as noted above. This was the case with Kyniska, who won as an owner of chariot teams, as is seen from the inscription on a base (390-380 B.C., left corner of the gallery).

The only woman known to have ignored the rule was the famous Kallipateira, daughter of the Rhodian boxer Diagoras, who came from a family of Olympic victors. Her father, her brother, her sons and nephews were all Olympic victors. When she went to take part in the games, her youngest son, Peisirodos, wanted to accompany her. So she disguised herself as a trainer (paidotribe) and entered the Stadium. Her son won and in her joy she leapt to embrace him. Then the chiton she was wearing fell down, exposing her as a woman. Even so, the Eleian judges did not punish the woman who came from a family of Olympic victors and had produced sons who were

Bronze strigils, 3rd century B.C. (Olympia, Archaeological Museum M 348, 281, 349).

Inscribed marble base of a statue of Damagetos, son of Diagoras, and Olympic victor in the 82nd and 83rd Olympics (452 and 448 B.C., Olympia Archaeological Museum OLV 152). The famous pankratiast, Diagoras, had three sons who were Olympic victors, Damagetos, Akousilaos and Dorieus. Standing beside the enormous statue of Diagoras in the Altis were the statues of his sons, Damagetos and Dorieus, victorious in the pankration, and Akousilaos, victorious in boxing. Only the base with the names of the victors has survived.

victorious in the Games. In the succeeding Games, however, they obliged trainers to enter the Stadium nude, just as the athletes.

The episode of Kallipateira has been uniquely immortalised in the moving sonnet of the modern Greek poet, Lorentzos Mavilis:

"How did you enter, Noble Lady of Rhodes?
Ancient custom bars women from entering
here." "I have a nephew, Eukleus, and
three brothers, son, father, all Olympic victors.
You must allow me, Hellanodikai,
so I too may admire in the beautiful bodies,
brave praiseworthy souls, who
for the wild olive of Herakles contend.
Do not compare me to other women,
In this age my house will brilliantly shine
with the unfading privileges of courage.
Written in gold my house is honoured
on a great block of bright marble
by the golden hymn of immortal Pindar."

Found in the Altis was the base of the statue of Diagoras and also the bases of the statues of Damagetos and Dorieus, his sons and the brothers of Kallipateira (wall opposite the entrance).

Women's athletics saw notable development in Greece in ancient times. Celebrated at Olympia were the Heraia, running races in honour of Hera. Hippodameia was supposed to have been the founder and to have run the first race with 16 other women. The maidens who ran in the races were divided into three groups according to age. They ran 5/6 ths of the Stadium course (160 m.), wearing a short chiton leaving the right shoulder exposed and their hair untied. The

prize was a crown of olive and a portion of the cow that was sacrificed to Hera. Characteristic is the bronze figure of the woman-
runner from Dodone (copy, middle of the 6th century B.C., left
case). As reported by Pausanias, the victors dedicated their portraits in the temple of Hera, where they were placed in shallow rectangular niches, still visible today in the columns of the colonnade.

Also displayed in the gallery are two statues of Eleian women
from the Heraion (2nd half of the 1st century A.C.), a small statue
of Athenaïs, daughter of Herodes Atticus, of the little Hereulanean
type (2nd half of the 2nd century A.C.) and a series of lekythoi with
chariot racing scenes.

Central gallery 6

Programme of the Games - the contests. The programme
of the Games did not remain unchanged during the historical course
of the institution, which lasted over a thousand years. In Classical
times it had become as described below.

Two days before the Games began, athletes, judges and officials
took part in a procession from Elis to Olympia along the Sacred Way.

On the morning of the first day, athletes, their relatives and the
judges gave the sacred oath that they would uphold the rules,
before the statue of Zeus Orkios (Zeus who presides over oaths)
in the Bouleuterion. The names of the athletes were then recorded, with their classification in the contests, and they were paired
or placed in order for competing, by lot. Flute contests and the
contests of the heralds were held near the entrance to the Stadium. In the evening sacrifices were made and oracles pronounced.
Philosophers, historians and poets recited their works to the
assembled crowd.

The second day saw the beginning of the Games with the running contest of the boys in the Stadium, followed by the boys'
wrestling, boxing and the pankration (both boxing and wrestling).

On the third day the chariot races and equestrian contests were
held in the Hippodrome. In the evening, in the Stadium, the pentathlon (jumping, diskos throwing, running, javelin throwing, wrestling)
took place. A black ram was sacrificed in the evening in honour of
Pelops, founder of the chariot contest, and this was followed by a
festival feast.

The fourth day, which coincided with the great summer full
moon, began with a stately procession. Athletes, Hellanidikai and
theoroi (state ambassadors) began at the Gymnasium or Prytaneion
and went to the great Altar of Zeus where 100 animals (hecatomb)

 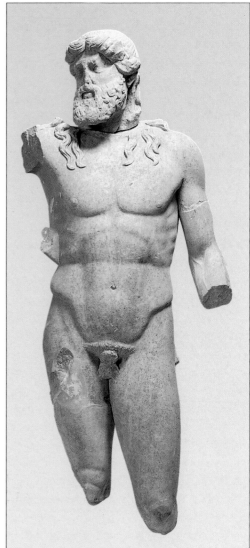

Bronze figure of a diskobolos. On the left side is an inscrip-
tion: TO ΔΙΓΟΣ ΙΜΙ. Together with the runner shown (B 26)
and three other statuettes of athletes (a jumper, a wrestler
and a javelin thrower), this was the dedication of a victor in
the pentathlon, 500-490 B.C. From an Argive workshop
(Olympia, Archaeological Museum B 6767+7500).

Statue of Zeus in Pentelic marble, part of the sculptural
decoration of the Nymphaion. It is a copy of the time of
Antoninus (2nd century A.C.) of a bronze original of 460
B.C., probably by the sculptor Myron (Olympia, Archaeologi-
cal Museum Λ 109).

were sacrificed. Then came the men's running races, wrestling, boxing and the pankration. The day ended with the hoplite races.

The fifth and final day of the Games was devoted to awarding the athletes. The victors went to the temple of Zeus, where they were crowned with wild olive (kotinos) by the most senior of the Hellanodikai. An official feast followed in the Prytaneion and there were festival celebrations lasting into the night.

The Olympic contests. While they were staying in Elis, the athletes were divided by the Hellanodikai into groups. The boys between 14 and 18 years belonged to the category of children (boys). The boys' Games were introduced in the 37th Olympiad (632 B.C.) when a third day was added to the Games. The boy's pentathlon was part of the programme only once, in the 38th Olympiad (628 B.C.).

Notable in this unit of the exhibition are two bronze figurines of runners and a bronze statuette of a diskos thrower, portrayed at the moment when he leans back to hurl the diskos that he holds in

Bronze figurine of a runner with a dedication, TO ΔIΦOΣ IMI, inscribed on the right thigh. It shows the athlete in motion (ca. 490 B.C.). It was dedicated by an Olympic victor and it is the product of an Argive workshop (Olympia, Archaeological Museum B 26).

One of the two little statues (now headless) of the goddess Tyche that were one on each side of the monumental propylon (entrance court) of the Krypte (the vaulted passageway to the Stadium). They were supposed to be with the athletes in their greatest test. The goddess holds her attributes, the measure and the rudder and she has a wheel as support. 2nd century A.C. (Olympia, Archaeol. Museum Λ 112).

Trefoil oinochoe depicting a chariot race, from Corinth, 500 B.C. (Athens, National Archaeological Museum AE 523).

his upraised right hand. Shown on an Attic red-figured kylix are two boys in a boxing match, in which one boy is in the position known as "*apagoreuein*", of giving up, having accepted his defeat.

Dedicatory bases of statues of boy-victors come from the Altis, such as the inscribed bases of Xenokles and Gorgias (2nd half of the 4th century B.C.) who won in wrestling. The bronze head of a boy is dated in late Hellenistic times and next to it is a modern copy. Next to these, an inscribed bronze plaque records that someone named Philip was a victor in the boys' wrestling competition (3rd century B.C.).

The right-hand long side of the gallery is devoted to sculpture. Notable are two small statues representing the goddess Tyche, the marble nude torso of a statue of a boy, torsos from statues of youths (ephebes), dedication bases in the form of Doric and Ionic column capitals, and the base of the dedication of Klaudia for the Olympic victory of her son Peisanos.

The equestrian contests. Equestrian contests were held for the first time in the 33rd Olympiad (648 B.C.) with the races of the magnificent riding horses, riding contests with the horse making 6 courses around the Hippodrome. In 496 B.C. (71st Olympiad) the mares' trotting race, the *kalpe*, was introduced and in 256 B.C. (131st Olympiad), the colt races. The horseman rode nude, without saddle-cloth, saddle or stirrups. The saddle-cloth appears to have been used only by the cavalry.

Notable among the exhibits connected with the equestrian contests are:

The inscribed base, in the form of a Doric capital, of Charops, victor in equestrian contests (1st century B.C.), an Attic black-figured krater showing a horse race, and a black-figured vase with representations of horsemen (6th century B.C.). Finally, bronze bridles, bronze and clay figurines of horses and riders are characteristic of the exhibits related to the equestrian contests.

The Chariot races. Tradition holds that the first chariot race was run between Pelops and Oinomaos.

The chariot races and the equestrian contests were the most impressive of the games and they were held in the Hippodrome. The chariot competitions at Olympia were as follows: four-horse chariot race with a course of twelve times around the Hippodrome; it was introduced in the 25th Olympiad (680 B.C.) and continued until A.D. 241. The contest known as the *apene*, in which a four-wheeled wagon was drawn by a pair of mules, was introduced in the 70th Olympiad (500 B.C.) and given up in 444 B.C. (84th Olympiad).

Attic red-figured kylix with the representation of a boxing match (ca. 500 B.C.). The defeated athlete has accepted defeat, assuming the conventional position with his pointing finger extended. This is the gesture that signifies the end of the contest (Athens, Agora Museum P 24110)

Clay statuette of a horseman, early 5th century B.C., from Rhitsona in Boiotia (Thebes, Archaeological Museum AE 6037).

Attic black-figured column-krater by the Louvre Painter, with a representation of a horse-race. 550-540 B.C. (Athens, National Archaeological Museum AE 11706).

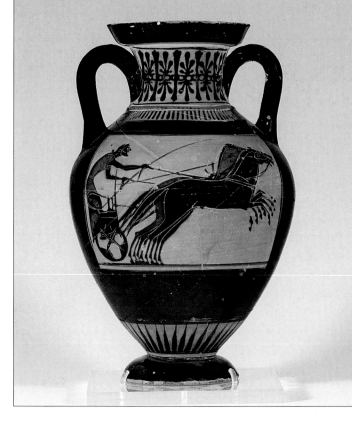

Pseudo-Panathenaic amphora showing a four-horse chariot, end of the 6th century B.C. (Athens, Agora Museum P 24661).

*Part of a marble dedicatory relief
with a four-horse chariot team,
end of the 4th century B.C.
(Larisa, Archaeological Museum
AE 79/119).*

The contest of the *synoris* (chariot drawn by a pair of horses) was
introduced in the 93rd Olympiad (408 B.C.). The contest of the four-
horse chariot drawn by foals had a course of 8 turns around the
Hippodrome; it was introduced in the 99th Olympiad (348 B.C.). The
synoris contest in which the chariot was drawn by a pair of foals had
a course of 3 wide turns around the Hippodrome, and was introduced in the 128th Olympiad (268 B.C.).

The victor of the contests was the owner of the horses and he
was crowned with a wreath of wild olive. The charioteer received a
woollen fillet, which was tied around his forehead by the owner of
the team. This is why women (Kyniska), children or even cities are
named as victors in the chariot races. Known names of charioteers
are Phintis the Syracusan, Karrotos (charioteer of Arkesilaos, king of
Cyrene), Chromios (charioteer of Hieron of Syracuse) and others.

The finds from the Sanctuary of Olympia that were dedicated to
Zeus bear witness to the long tradition of chariot racing in the
place. The large iron chariot wheel is impressive. To be seen as well

Representation of a long jump. The jumper uses his weights (halters) for impetus in the take-off. When he reaches the sill or threshold he swings the weights backwards and forwards, making his jump with the forward swing. Slightly before he lands he throws the weights behind him (drawing by K. Iliadis, Ekdotike Athenon archive).

are the bronze figurines of charioteers, bronze strips of the 6th century B.C. preserving scenes of chariot racing, and pottery, like the pseudo-Panathenaic amphorae, kylikes, oinochoai, lekythoi (5th century B.C.) with similar scenes. On a fragment of a marble dedicatory relief with a representation of a four-horse chariot, the horses are rendered naturalistically and full of power.

The pentathlon. Five contests made up the pentathlon: jumping, running, throwing the javelin, the diskos and wrestling. The first three were considered light sport, the final two, heavy. According to tradition, Jason established the pentathlon (combination of five contests) in honour of his friend Paleas, who had won in wrestling in the games held by the Argonauts in Lemnos, but had come in second in all the other contests. The pentathlon was introduced in the 18th Olympiad (708 B.C.).

Jumping, the javelin throw and the diskos throw were contests held only as part of the pentathlon, whereas running and wrestling were held also as separate contests with separate prizes. Aristotle considered the victor of the pentathlon to be "the best of the Greeks". The manner in which the pentathlon was proclaimed is still unknown.

The jump. This took place in the Stadium in a "*skamma*", a rectangular pit or "dug-up", 50 feet (16 m.) long, filled with sand. On one side was the "threshold" or sill (for the take-off), and where the athlete's feet touched down on the sand after his jump, they placed a marker and measured the result by means of a wooden rod known

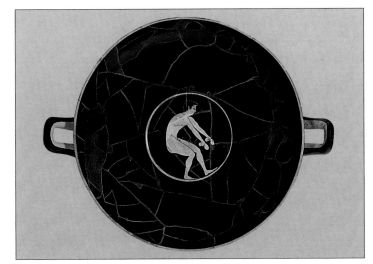

Attic red-figured kylix by the Epeleios Painter, showing an athlete jumping (Athens, Agora Museum P 24068).

Stone dedicatory jumping weight of the Spartan Akmatis (550-525 B.C.). The dedicatory inscription says that Akmatis won without getting "sandy", either because his opponent did not appear, or because his opponent recognized the superiority of Akmatis and declined the contest. The halter weighs 4.629 milligrams (Olympia, Archaeological Museum Λ 189).

Attic red-figured lekythos by the Pinakis Painter, showing an athlete practicing for the javelin throw. 3rd quarter of the 5th century B.C. From Eretria (Athens, National Archaeological Museum AE 12781).

as a "canon". The expression "to jump beyond the skamma" referred to the athletes who jumped beyond the end of the sand-pit. This was the origin of the saying "to surpass what is dug", an expression still used in modern Greek today, in a metaphorical sense.

For a better result in the long jump, the athletes used *halteres*, jumping weights of stone or lead. There were various types, elliptical, amphi-spherical, but basically they were either long or spherical. The weights that have survived weigh 1.610, 1.480 or 2.018 or even as much as 4.629 gr. The extremely heavy weights were dedicatory. Depending on their build, the jumpers used the suitable sort of weight, but their use was not obligatory. The athletes used the weights also for exercising their hands, their arms and their fingers (*halterobolia*).

The jump was probably simple, double or triple, since jumps are recorded up to 16,66 m. The performance of the contest was accompanied by the aulos, since music helped the jumper to have rhythm. The heroic Phaullos of Kroton, who fought at Salamis, was legendary, for he jumped 55 feet (16,28 m.). So too Chionis the Lakedaimonian (664 B.C.), who reached 52 feet (16,66 m.) On the pottery displayed here (bell krater and a kylix of the 4th and 6th centuries B.C.) jumpers are depicted in the course of the contest.

Notable among the jumping weights is the stone weight of Akmatis with a dedicatory inscription (end of the 6th century B.C.). The exhibition unit is completed by a base of dark stone with an inscription recording the victory of Pythokles in the pentathlon.

The diskos. Homer calls the diskos a *solos* (a weight that was looped with a strap and shot out, like the modern sling stone). It was introduced at Olympia in 632 B.C. as part of the pentathlon. Initially the diskos was of stone, later on it was also made of bronze, lead or iron. Those preserved have a diameter ranging from 0,17 to 0,35 m. and weigh between 1.300 and 6.600 gr. The largest ones were dedicatory. Apart from inscriptions, representations could be etched on the surface of the diskos, usually of athletes, or else an ode or covenant was copied, such as the covenant of the sacred truce.

The technique of the competition did not differ greatly from the game of today. At the position of the throw, stakes or nails were driven into the ground, called markers ("*semeia*"). The distance of the throw was measured with a pole or string. For the competition, the same diskos was used by all the athletes. Pausanias (VI,19,4) notes that 3 official diskoi were kept at Olympia in the Treasury of the Sikyonians for the pentathlon. Phaullos of Kroton was a great diskos thrower (with a record of 96 feet or 28,10 m.) and Phlegias of Pisa threw a diskos across the widest part of the Alpheios river bed, from one bank to the other.

Inscribed bronze diskos dedicated by Poplios Asklepias, victor in the pentathlon. On one side, the inscription says that the dedication was made by Poplios Asklepias the Corinthian as a thanks offering. The other side records the validation of the official to whom the offering was entrusted. A.D. 241 (Olympia, Archaeological Museum M 891).

Attic red-figured kylix showing a diskobolos (diskos thrower), 480 B.C. (Athens, Agora Museum P 2698).

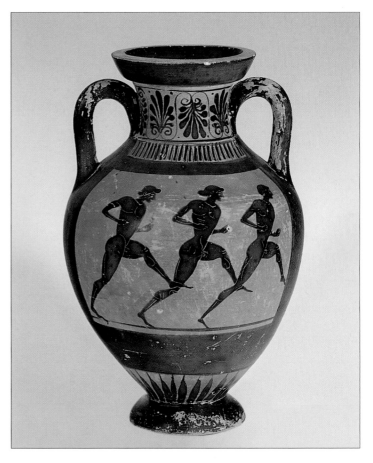

Attic black-figured pseudo-pana-thenaic amphora by the Oxford Painter (500 B.C.), with a representation of runners in the dolichos or long-distance race (Rhodes, Archaeological Museum AE 13281).

The stone seat of the Lakedai-monian ambassador Gorgos was found in the archaic Stadium of Olympia. It bears the inscription ΛΑΚΕΔΑΙΜΟΝΙΟΣ ΠΡΟΞΕΝΟΣ FΑΛΕΙΩΝ, 2nd half of the 6th century-early 5th century B.C. (Olympia, Archaeological Museum Λ 192).

The bronze diskoi on display here all come from Olympia. The large inscribed diskos is a dedication of Poplios Asklepias, victor in the pentathlon that was held in A.D. 241. On both sides there are inscriptions. Representations of diskos throwers are shown also on pottery.

The javelin. The contest has its origin in hunting and war. There were two types of javelin throw: distance throwing, and target throwing at a predetermined mark. In the pentathlon at Olympia, the competition was for distance only.

The javelin was a long wooden pole of 1,50 - 2 m. with a sharp point at one end. For the target throw a metal point was used. At the centre of gravity of the pole a leather throwing-thong (the *amentum* or *ankyle*) was attached, forming a loop in which the thrower placed his first and middle fingers. The technique of hurling the javelin was no different from that of today.

Displayed in the thematic unit of the javelin are four bronze spearheads of Archaic times and an Attic red-figured lekythos with a scene showing the training of a javelin thrower (5th century B.C.).

The foot race. This was the oldest and most important of the Olympic Games. The victor in the stade race gave his name to the Olympiad.

The creators of the competition were supposed to have been the Idaian Herakles and the Kouretes, the famous hero, Herakles, and others. The runners ran bare-footed and initially they wore a *perizoma* or loin-girdle. Tradition has it that in the 15th Olympiad (720 B.C.), Orsippos of Megara, in the course of the race, let his *perizoma* fall and continued running completely nude. Orsippos won and, from then on, it was decided that the athletes should run in the contest nude. Famous runners were Leonidas the Rhodian, who won 4 successive Olympiads (154th - 157th, 164-152 B.C.), Ergomenes the Xanthian and others.

The following foot races were held in the Olympic Games:

The stade: a sprint or speed race of one stade (600 feet = 192,27 m.) which is the equivalent of the modern 200 m. race. The victor was known as the *stadionikes* or stade victor. The first stade victor at Olympia was Koroibos the Eleian. Until the 13th Olympiad (728 B.C.), the stade was the only competition in the Games.

The diaulos: speed race, a double course, once up, once down, of 1200 feet, corresponding to the modern 400 m. race. The *diaulos* was introduced into the Olympic Games in the 14th Olympiad (724 B.C.).

The dolichos: the long-distance race, an endurance race of 7 to 24 stades. In most cases the distance was set at 20 stades, thus

A looped leather thong or amentum was fastened at the centre of gravity of the javelin. The javelin thrower inserted one or two fingers into the loop to give the throw greater momentum (drawing by K Iliadis, Ekdotike Athenon archive).

3.550-3.800 m. The competition was introduced in the 15th Olympiad (720 B.C), with Akanthos the Lakonian as first victor.

The hoplite race: a speed race between 2 and 4 stades (usually 2) in length, in which the athlete runs the course wearing defensive panoply (helmet, greaves, shield). It was introduced at Olympia in 520 B.C. (65th Olympiad). The hoplite race is thought to have been a funerary race in honour of a dead hero.

The horse-race: a medium course of four stades that was not run at Olympia, but was included in the Isthmian, Nemean and Panathenaic Games.

Displayed in the unit of foot races are black-figured pottery (lekythoi, kraters and amphorae) of the 6th century B.C. that illustrate runners. Other works included in the unit are: a statue of an athlete from ancient Messene (copy), a portrait of an athlete from Corinth, a fragment of a stone starting-post from the archaic Stadium of Olympia and two thrones that were honorary seats. One was for the Lakedaimonian ambassador, the other for Euphanios.

Wrestling. Identified as founders of the competition are Hermes, Theseus in his fight with Kerkyon, Herakles when he was victorious against the giants Antaios, Achelloos, Triton and various monsters, and Palaistra, daughter of Hermes.

Wrestling was added to the Olympic Games in the 18th Olympiad (708 B.C.). The boys' wrestling competition was included from 632 B.C. (37th Olympiad) on.

There were two styles of wrestling, upright wrestling (ὀρθὴ πάλη or σταδαία πάλη) and ground wrestling (ἀλίνδησις or κύλισις). In the first the object was simply to throw the opponent three times to the ground. In the second, after the first fall, the fight continued on the ground until one or the other admitted defeat by taking the position known as "apagoreuein", a position signifying defeat. The wrestlers' opponents (5 to 8) were chosen by lot.

The wrestlers fought in a sand-pit, their bodies oiled and naked. Details about the contest are provided by the many scenes on pottery and by the bronze figurines representing wrestlers. Among the wrestlers that achieved fame were Milon of Kroton, who won 6 times at Olympia, 7 in the Pythian Games, 9 at Nemea and 10 at Isthmia, and Hipposthenes the Spartan, with 6 victories at Olympia.

One of the decorated bronze shield-bands (6th century B.C.) exhibited here, has a representation of wrestlers. Likewise of interest is a bronze group of wrestlers of Roman times, from Egypt. The base with the sole of the foot remains from a bronze statue of the wrestler and pankratiast Kapros (late 3rd century B.C.). Included

Bronze pair of wrestlers, from Egypt, Roman period. Notable is the similarity of the hand-grips to those used by wrestlers today (Athens, National Archaeological Museum, Demetriadis Collection AIΓ 2547).

also in this unit is a stone of 143,5 k., which Bibon lifted with one hand, as we learn from the inscription.

Boxing. According to mythology, Apollo was the initiator of boxing. But Herakles and Theseus and other heroes as well are credited with the idea. Be that as it may, the protector of the competition was thought to be Apollo.

The competition was introduced in the 23rd Olympiad (688 B.C.) and, in the 41st Olympiad (616 B.C.), boys' boxing was added.

The contenders fought until one of them fell unconscious or acknowledged defeat. Pairing of the boxers was by lot.

For the match, the athletes wore thongs around their hands, a

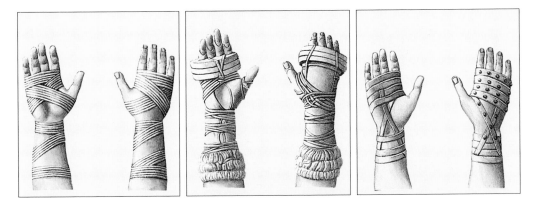

Drawing showing the development of the himantes or gloves worn by boxers. Initially they consisted of leather thongs ("soft gloves"). In the 4th century they were replaced by a kind of glove ("sharp gloves") and in Roman times the caestus, a boxing glove reinforced with iron or lead, came into use (drawing by K. Iliadis, Ekdotike Athenon archive).

Attic black-figured pseudo-panathenaic amphora from Tanagra, 500 B.C., showing a boxing match (Athens, National Archaeological Museum 402).

Bybon's stone, late 7th-early 6th century B.C. Inscribed in boustrophedon on the upper surface is ΒΥΒΩΝ ΤΕΤΕΡΕΙ ΧΕΡΙ ΥΠΕΡΚΕΦΑΛΑ Μ ΥΠΕΡΒΑΛΕΤΟ Ο ΦΟ[Λ]Α, "With one hand Bybon lifted me above his head". Weight lifting was not one of the Olympic contests (Olympia, Archaeological Museum Λ 191).

protection in use as early as Myceaean times. Homer describes them as thongs of ox-hide, which were wound around the boxers hands. Later on, hard leather thongs were added around the lower part of the fingers and wool was placed on the inside (known as *sphairai*). From the 4th century B.C. to the end of the 2nd century A.C., instead of thongs, the boxers wore a sort of glove. Finally, a heavy glove reinforced with lead and iron and known as the *caestus*, was prevalent in Roman times.

Among the most famous boxers of antiquity was Diagoras the Rhodian, father of Kallipateira, known as the "straight puncher", because he fought his opponents frontally.

The vases exhibited here depict boxing scenes. Characteristic is a kylix by the Heidelberg painter from ancient Corinth (560 B.C.) and an Attic black-figured amphora from Tanagra in Boiotia (500 B.C.). The unit is completed with shield-bands with depictions of boxers, inscribed bases for statues of boxers who won in the Olympic Games, such as Euthymos the Lokrian (472 B.C.) and Kinyskos (middle of the 5th century B.C.), both found in the Altis, and the head of a statue of an athlete from Rhodes (early 3rd century B.C.).

The pankration. One of the most spectacular of the games was the pankration, a combination of boxing and wrestling. The tradition was that Theseus combined wrestling and boxing in order to overcome the Minotaur. It was introduced at Olympia in the 33rd Olympiad (648 B.C.).

The pankration was of two sorts: the upright pankration (the athletes fought upright) and the ground pankration (the opponents fell and continued on the ground). In training, the athletes usually practiced the upright type, but in the actual contest, they will have fought on the ground. The pankratiasts had to combine simultaneously the skills of both wrestler and boxer and the contest was strictly controlled by regulations. Among the famous pankratiasts were Lygdamis

Marble torso of a Kouros with the inscription ΑΡΡΑΧΙΩΝ ΦΙΓΑΛΕΙΕΥΣ, Archaic (2nd quarter of the 6th century B.C.). It belonged to Arrhachion of Phigaleia (in the district of Olympia), who was victorious in the pankration (wrestling and boxing), but died from a blow in the throat, whereas his opponent had already admitted defeat (Olympia, Archaeological Museum Λ 257).

Marble head of a pankratist or wrestler. It shows the influence of the schools of Skopas and Lysippos, ca. 340 B.C. (Olympia, Archaeological Museum Λ 99).

the Syracusan (first Olympic victor in the pankration in 648 B.C.), Sostratos the Sikyonian, Dorieus and Eukles (son and nephew respectively of Diagoras of Rhodes), and Polydamas the Skotoussaian.

Of the many statues of pankratiasts in the Altis, only a few bases have survived. Here we may see the bases of the statues of the pankratiast Kallias (472 B.C.) and of the great pankratiast Polydamas (2nd half of the 4th century B.C.), the last work of the famous Sikyonian sculptor Lysippos. The base shows in relief some of the accomplishments of the great athlete.

A Kouros from Phigaleia portrays the pankratiast Arrhachion who, although he died, was proclaimed victor because his opponent had already assumed the position of defeat.

Datable to around 340 B.C. is the head of a victor, probably in the pankration. The parted lips, the turn of the head and the eyes,

Statue of a heroized man, copy of an original of the 4th century B.C. of the type of the Hermes Richelieu in the Louvre (1st century A.C., Olympia, Archaeological Museum Λ 132+137).

Base of the statue of the Olympic pankratist Polydamas. The athlete's fame had spread beyond the limits of the ancient Greek world and the king of Persia, Dareios Ochos, invited him to Susa. There he competed with three chosen foot-soldiers and he beat them all. His portrait statue at Olympia, of which only the base has survived, was by the famous sculptor Lysippos. On the front of the base Dareios is shown with four women, watching Polydamas who has lifted his opponent in the air. Shown on the short sides of the base, the athlete is depicted as another Herakles, fighting a lion and sitting on the defeated animal (2nd half of the 4th century B.C., Olympia, Archaeological Museum Λ 45).

Marble dedicatory relief showing Nike crowning an athlete (410 B.C., Athens, Acropolis Museum AE 1329).

Sherd from a lekythos showing a hoplite runner. The athlete, wearing helmet and greaves and carrying his shield, is shown running. The hoplite race, one of the most difficult of the races, was originally a funerary race (Olympia, Archaeological Museum Π 1674).

placed deeply in their sockets, show clearly the influence of the schools of Skopas and Lysippos.

The hoplite race completes the list of Games. Pausanias reports that kept in the temple of Zeus at Olympia were 25 bronze shields that were meted out to the hoplites for use in the contest.

On display are greaves, helmets and shields of Archaic times. Especially impressive is a dedicatory shield decorated with a rhomboid pattern, found in the Altis. A red-figured Lekythos sherd preserves the figure of a hoplite runner.

Displayed in the gallery is also a statue base shaped like an astragalos. It was found in Olympia. The statue represented *"Kairos"*, "Opportunity" and it was a work by Poykleitos the Elder (5th century B.C.).

The nude male statue, half of which has survived, represents Hermes, or a hero, and it is Julio-Claudian in date.

Gallery 7

The victors of the Games. The prize of the Games, which were known as *"stephanites"* or "games in which the prize was a stephane", was a stephane or wreath of wild olive, the *kotinos*. It was the greatest honour given by the gods to man. Tradition has it that the *kotinos* was established as the prize of the Games by Iphitos, following a relevant Delphic oracle. The olive branches for crowning the victor were taken from the *"Kallistephanos elaia"*, the "beautiful-crowned olive" that grew near the SW corner of the temple of Zeus. The branches were cut with a golden sickle by a young boy, whose parents both were living. The crowns were then placed on

Kolotes' gold and ivory table, which was taken to the temple of Zeus. From there the Hellanodikai took it for the crowning ceremony. The victors arrived at the temple decked with the symbols of victory, a fillet of purple wool bound around the head, and carrying a palm branch. The spectators showered them with flowers and leaves, and shouted out the verses of Archilochos' hymn "Τήνελλα Καλλίνικε", "Well done, glorious athlete". The importance of a victory at Olympia was immeasurable. The Olympic victor was the "chosen" of the gods. His perpetual fame was his greatest reward. These victories were immortalized by the great poets, such as Simonides, Bacchylides and, greatest of them all, Pindar.

Bronze coin of the Eleians, 2nd century A.C. The reverse shows the gold and ivory table, made by the sculptor Kolotes, on which the kotinoi (the wild olive crowns) were placed prior to crowning the Olympic victors (Olympia, Archaeological Museum M 876).

Displayed in the unit devoted to the victory of the athletes are: a marble dedicatory relief (410 B.C.) showing a Nike crowning a victorious athlete, two terracotta statues of Nike, preserved in fragments, from the Altis, and part of a mosaic floor showing Nike crowning a personification of Agon, the Contest (left part of the gallery).

On a red-figured calyx-krater there is an impressive scene of a

Terracotta statue of Nike, from the akroterion of a building. It is a fine example of the plastic art of Olympia, ca. 500-490 B.C., Olympia, Archaeological Museum T 304 - T 254).

Red-figured kalyx-krater by the Athens Painter (370-360 B.C.) showing Nike in a four-horse chariot. (Athens, National Archaeological Museum AE 12250).

Bronze figurine of an athlete. He his depicted crowned and is of the Kouros type. Product of a Lakonian workshop, middle of the 6th century B.C. (Olympia, Archaeological Museum B 2400).

four-horse chariot being driven by Nike (370-360 B.C.). On display also are a considerable number of vases with representations of Nike, a bronze figurine of a crowned athlete and part of a bronze relief with a figure of Nike from the Altis. The table of Kolotes, made of wood, gold and ivory, on which the crowns were placed before the crowning ceremony, was kept in the Heraion. The table did not survive. In addition to Pausanias' valuable description, it appears on the reverse of a coin of A.D. 133 from Olympia, the obverse of which shows a bust of Hadrian. Bronze inscriptions mention the victors of the Games, such as a fragment of an inscribed plaque from the Altis recording the victory of Ergoteles (right-hand case).

In the centre of the gallery stands a small plaster model of the Nike of Paionios. It was made in bronze in 1919 by the sculptor Michalis Tombros, at the request of Eleutherios Venizelos, who wanted it given on his behalf to the French commander-in-chief, General Louis-François d'Esperé.

Part of a mosaic floor with a representation of Nike crowning the personification of Agon (Contest), 5th century A.C. (Larisa, Archaeological Museum ΜΛ/ΨΙ).

A composition of olive leaves in bronze. The leaves came from the kotinos and the Olympic victors dedicated them in the Sanctuary of Zeus (Olympia, Archaeological Museum).

Handle of a bronze tripod lebes (1st half of the 8th century B.C.). The handle is decorated with incised geometrical patterns and is crowned by a little horse. The lebes, in Homer's time the most highly valued of competition prizes, was the most favoured dedication at the Sanctuary of Zeus in Geometric and Archaic times (Olympia, Archaeological Museum Br. 9694).

Representation of an athlete on a vase in the Hermitage Museum of St Petersburg. Red woollen fillets have been tied around the athlete's upper arm and thigh. Immediately following a victory at Olympia, the Hellanodikai gave the victors the symbols of their victory: they gave them the palm branch to hold and they tied purple wool fillets around their heads.

Gallery 8

Prizes - votive offerings. The Olympic victor received great honours on his return to his city. Part of the city walls were torn down so that the victor could enter with his four-horse chariot, if the city who produced the Olympic victor had no need of its fortification. The victor then offered sacrifices to the divinity who protected the city, and to whom he dedicated his stephane. A festival feast followed, attended by all the citizens of the city.

Another privilege acquired by the victor was to be fed at public expense for the rest of his life, relief from all taxes, and participation in the Boule. In Athens, Solon instituted also a monetary prize. In Sparta the victor won the right to fight beside the king. At all

*Portrait of Nero (54-68 A.C.).
In the Olympic Games of A.D. 67,
organized by the Roman emperor himself and known as the
False Olympic Games, he claimed
victory in 6 contests from which
he obliged his opponents to
withdraw (Elis, Archaeological
Museum Λ 333).*

*Silver tetradrachm of the Syracusans (485-465 B.C.). A chariot
with charioteer is depicted on
the reverse (Athens, Numismatic
Museum, 1910/II, KE´4).*

public events Olympic victors had a place of honour and their names were recorded on stelai.

In some cities, the Olympic victors were worshipped as heroes after death. Yet the greatest honour was the victory ode, the poem of praise written in celebration of the victory, for the Olympic victors were "*aoidimoi*", famous in song, worthy of the poems written. They had also the right to erect their statues in the sacred Altis. Pausanias records the presence of 230 such statues in the Sanctuary at Olympia. These high honours secured the glory of the Olympic victor and his immortality through the ages. In the 4th century B.C., the sophist Hippias brought the list of Olympic victors up to date, on the basis of the Sanctuary archive. Later on, others did the same. Today we know the names of 922 people who were victorious in the Olympic Games.

Exhibited in this gallery are bronze tripod legs and decorative lebes handles of Geometric times, and a reproduction of a bronze lebes or cauldron. The floor of the gallery is taken up by a copy of a mosaic from Patras. Depicted on it are athletes, musicians, poets and dramatic competitions (late 2nd - early 3rd century A.C.). Finds from the excavations at Olympia include bronze leaves, branches and olives, of various sizes, from the dedicatory *kotinos* or wild olive of the athletes. This shows the tremendous importance of the *kotinos* as a symbol inseparably tied to the Olympic ideal and as the highest reward for the *agon*, or struggle, of the athlete.

Gallery 9

A. The spectators of the Games. From the very borders of the ancient Greek world came thousands of pilgrims to watch the Games. The various cities sent their ambassadors, their *theoria* or sacred embassy, led by the architheoros or chief of the embassy. They all stayed in tents set up along the banks of the two rivers, the Alpheios and the Kladeos, or simply beneath the trees.

Famous orators (Gorgias, Lysias, Demosthenes, Isokrates), philosophers (Anaxagoras, Sokrates, Plato, Aristotle), historians (Herodotos), politicians, sculptors and creators of bronze statues (Polykleitos, Lysippos) and others came to see the Games and to show their works. Thales the Milesian, one of the seven wise men of ancient Greece, breathed his last in the Stadium while he was watching the Games. On entering the Stadium after the victory of the Greeks against the Persians at Salamis (480 B.C.), Themistokles was practically deified and the spectators stopped shouting their praises of the athletes. At Olympia Isokrates explained his "Panhellenic Idea".

Marble head of Alexander the Great, copy of a 4th century original. It is attributed to Lysippos since it is rendered with the known characteristics of Lysippan work (tilt of the head, eyes looking dramatically upwards, wavy hair, parted lips and a line across the forehead) and because Lysippos had the privilege of being the only sculptor allowed to make portraits of Alexander (Olympia, Archaeological Museum Λ 246).

B. Hellenistic and Roman times.

During Hellenistic times, the Games became more cosmopolitan and professional athletics made their appearance. Roman times saw the beginning of their decline. In the 2nd century A.C., when the right of Roman citizenship was given to all the inhabitants of the Roman Empire, the Games assumed an international character that was retained after their revival. Sovereigns and emperors coveted the Olympic victory as a means of projecting and establishing their power and they minted coins on the occasion of their victories. After Philip II of Macedonia, the emperor Tiberius won the four-horse chariot race (4 B.C.), Germanicus won in A.D.17 and Nero (21lth Olympiad) won in 6 contests after obliging his opponents to withdraw. Despite continuous blows, the Olympic Games continued until A.D. 393, when they were stopped by the edict of Theodosios I.

On exhibit in the Gallery is a marble head of Alexander from Alpheiousa (area of Olympia), a portrait statue of the Roman

Gold stater of Philip II, from Pella. It is an issue commemorating the victory of the Macedonian king in the chariot race of 352 or 348 B.C. at Olympia. On the obverse is the head of Apollo, on the reverse a synoris or biga with charioteer and the inscription ΦΙΛΙΠΠΟΥ (340-328 B.C., Athens, Numismatic Museum AE 1400).

Head of a wrestler, with the features of Antinoos, the favourite of Hadrian (117-138 A.C., Olympia, Archaeological Museum Λ 104+208).

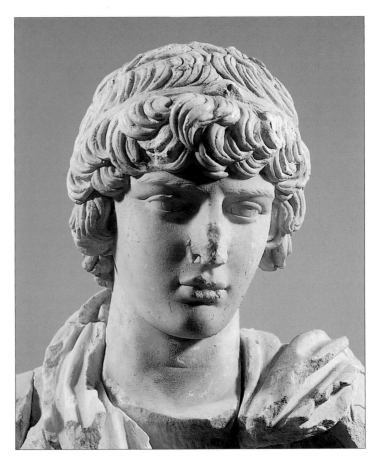

emperor Claudius (41-54 A.C.), a statue of an athlete of Roman times, identified by many as Antinoos, and a portrait of Nero.

Coins are displayed in a small case. Noteworthy among them are a gold stater of Philip II, king of Macedonia, and a silver tetradrachm of the Syracusans.

Panhellenic Games

In places where local games had been held for a dead hero in Mycenaean times, there the great Panhellenic Sanctuaries developed and Panhellenic Games were held in honour of a god. The funerary games of prehistoric times assumed a purely religious character and athletics became an inseparable part of Greek education. As early as the 8th century B.C., historic figures reorganized the Games in the Panhellenic Sanctuaries (Olympia, Delphi, Nemea, Isthmia). The cohesion of the Greeks as an ethnos was of great significance for the Panhellenic Games, in which they acquired the feeling of a common identity.

The two last galleries of the Museum are devoted to the other

Panhellenic Games, with objects that come from various other Greek Museums.

Gallery 10

The Pythia. The Pythia were held at Delphi, in the cult centre of Apollo. Tradition holds that it was Apollo himself who established the games when he killed the frightful snake Python.

The ancient Pythian games were held every eight years and they were solely musical competitions. The first reorganization after the First Sacred War of 582 B.C., is attributed to the Kleisthenes, tyrant of Sikyon. At that time, race-course and equestrian games were added, on the model of the Olympic Games. The games were then held every five years, with four years in between, in the month of Boukation (August-September).

Marble portrait statue of the emperor Claudius (41-54 B.C.) depicted as Zeus. Found in the Metroon (Olympia, Archaeological Museum Λ 125).

The prize was a wreath of laurel from Apollo's sacred tree.

With the proclamation of the Pythian Games, the sacred Pythia began. This lasted for a year, during which time the Greeks were forbidden to take hostage or to rob the *theoroi* (sacred embassies) or the pilgrims.

The games came to an end in A.D. 393 with the edict of Theodosios the Great.

The objects displayed in the gallery of the Pythian Games include: a black-figured olpe with a representation of Apollo (510-500 B.C.) from Kameiros in Rhodes, a statuette of a Kouros from Delphi (530-520 B.C.), the inscribed rim of a bronze lebes, which was a victory prize dedicated in the Delphic Sanctuary (530-520 B.C.), and two inscribed stone statue bases.

Gallery II

A. The Isthmia. The Isthmia were the third most important of the Panhellenic Games and were held every two years at the end of April in the Sanctuary of Poseidon, in honour of the god. They were reorganized along the lines of the Olympic Games in 582 B.C. In addition to race-course and equestrian contests, there were "contests of the young men", which comprised a kind of rowing race, music competitions and painting competitions. The victor's prize was a wreath of pine and later on of celery. The Corinthians ran these games until the 1st century B.C. With the destruction of Corinth in 146 B.C. by the Romans, the Sanctuary of Poseidon at Isthmia was abandoned and the games transferred to Sikyon.

From the Sanctuary of Poseidon at Isthmia come some iron scrapers or strigils of the 4th century B.C., one stone and one lead halter (jumping weights, Hellenistic and 6th century B.C. respectively), and a copy of a bronze statuette of Poseidon from Pella, of Hellenistic date (left-hand part of the gallery).

The Nemea or **Nemeia.** The Nemea were held in honour of Zeus in his Sanctuary at Nemea. Tradition has it that the founder of the games was Herakles, who established them after his first labour at Nemea. Written tradition, however, tells a different tale: that the Nemea were established in 573 B.C. in honour of Zeus.

The games were held every two years and, until the end of the 5th century B.C., they were held at Nemea. After the destruction of the temple of Zeus, until 330 B.C., they were held at Argos. In 145 B.C., the Roman Mummius returned the games to Nemea. The contests comprised the stadium competitions, the *dolichos* or long

Marble relief depicting the labours of Herakles (Lion of Nemea, Lernaian Hydra and Kerberos), 2nd century A.C. (Athens, National Archaeological Museum AE 4484).

race (12 stades), the *diaulos* (double course), wrestling, the pankration, the pentathlon, the hoplite race, riding and chariot races. Musical competitions were added in Hellenistic times. The prize was a stephane or crown of wild celery.

One of the best preserved stadia of the 4th century B.C. has been found at Nemea. It is curved at one end (*sphendone*) and the starting system has survived.

Notable among the objects exhibited in this unit is the 2nd century B.C. relief showing the labours of Herakles: the Lion of Nemea, the Lernaian Hydra and Kerberos. It comes from the ancient deme of Acharnai in Attica (right-hand section of the gallery).

Part of a decree relief depicting Athena seated. End of the 5th - beginning of the 4th century B.C. (Athens, Acropolis Museum AE 2439+2937).

B. The Panathenaia. Apart from the great Panhellenic Games, many cities had local games that were connected with cult festivals. In these local games the prize was an object of value, such as gold stephanai, bronze tripods or some local product (for ex. olive oil) or material good.

The most important local games were the Panathenaia in Athens, which comprised the Greater and Lesser Panathenaia and were held in honour of Athena. The contests were the known Olympic games, but others were included, such as torch races, rowing and music contests.

In the Museum unit of the Panathenaia, the emphasis is on the

Panathenaic amphora from Eretria with a representation of wrestlers and winged Nike hovering above them, 360-359 B.C. (Eretria, Archaeological Museum ME 14815).

figure of the goddess Athena. She is shown as Promachos on a relief from the Acropolis (500 B.C.), seated on a fragment of a decree relief, likewise from the Acropolis (late 5th - early 4th century B.C., and standing on some impressive Panathenaic amphorae, prizes won in the Panathenaia. Three of these Panathenaic amphorae are exhibited in the gallery (from Eretria, Olynthos and Rheneia).

Athens held games in honour of Dionysos as well, known as the Oschophoria, and there were the Theseia in honour of Theseus, and the Herakleia in honour of Herakles. In Hellenistic times, many cities organized local games with the Olympic Games as their model.

Central Gallery of the Old Museum with the exhibition of the pediments.

Drawing by H. Haeberlin (1876) showing the workers in the first excavations of the Sanctuary.

MUSEUM OF THE HISTORY OF THE EXCAVATIONS AT OLYMPIA

Local workmen wearing the traditional attire, the tsolia, during the first excavations at Olympia. Photographic archive of the German Archaeological Institute.

Beside the Museum of the History of the Olympic Games in Antiquity is the old Ephoreion. This provided a place to stay for the Archaeological Ephors and for other archaeologists who worked from time to time at Olympia. In 2004 the building was renovated and transformed into an exhibition hall for the History of the Excavations of the Sanctuary of Olympia. Through photographs and visual material, the visitor can follow the history of the systematic excavation of Olympia, which was one of the three earliest such excavations to be carried out in Greece (with the Dipylon and Mycenae). It provided an example for excavations to come.

After the two powerful earthquakes of the 6th century A.C., the Sanctuary was a vast wasteland. Gradually it was buried by landslides from the Kronion hill and by the flooding and silting of the river Alpheios, while all the western part was carried away by the Kladeos torrent. The venerable Sanctuary slipped slowly into oblivion. Even the name of the area was changed, and the toponyms "Antilalos", "Serbia" and "Serbiana" took its place. A Venetian map of 1516 finally shows the confluence of the Kladeos with the Alpheios and, in the 18th century students of the ancient Greek texts sought the place of the much-sung Sanctuary. In 1767, special interest in Olympia was shown by J. J. Winckelmann, founder of modern archaeological research. He himself wanted to be the excavator of Olympia, but his plans were cut short by his murder.

The first to locate the Sanctuary was R. Chandler, an English traveller who visited Olympia in 1766. Soon afterwards, iin 1780, L. S. F. Fauvel arrived at the sacred site. He drew the first plans and, in 1799, was followed by the French traveller F.C.H.L. Pouqueville. In 1806 the first trial trench was made in the temple of Zeus by E. Dodwell and W. Gell and, in 1811, C. R. Cockerell and C. Haller von Hallerstein made a small excavation. The first plan of Olympia using the trigonometric method was prepared in 1813 by Allason and J. Spencer Stanhope.

In 1829, shortly after liberation from the Turks and the foundation of the Greek State, the first excavation was carried out, for a period of two months, by the French scientific mission (Expédition Scientifique de Morée), led by General N. J. Maison, with A. Blouet and J. J. Dubois. The temple of Zeus was discovered and the first finds came to light, including metope fragments that were taken to France and displayed in the Louvre.

Systematic excavation of the Sanctuary began in 1875, after efforts over the years by E. Curtius of the German Archaeological Institute, with an agreement signed by the Greek and German states, defining the terms and obligations of each. The first excavation period, during which most of the buildings were discovered, lasted from 1875 to 1881 and was carried out by E. Curtius, F. Adler, W. Dörpfeld, C. A. Boetticher, R. Borrmann, A. Furtwängler, G. Treu and P. Graef. The first results were published in the big five-volume work "OLYMPIA". A second excavation period followed, lasting from 1906 to 1929, with W. Dörpfeld in charge and the results were published in the two-volume work ALT-OLYMPIA. From 1937 to 1942, excavations were concentrated on the Stadium, with E. Kunze and H. Schleif in charge. With the 2nd world war, excavations were halted in 1942 and the site itself suffered great damage under the army of occupation. Post-war research began in 1952 under the supervision of E. Kunze and A. Mallwitz. Almost all the Sanctuary had by now been revealed.

Recent decades have brought to light large building complexes of Roman times. Under way at present are small-scale excavations and restoration by the German Archaeological Institute, under the supervision of the Ministry of Culture and the local Archaeological Ephorate. Results of the research are published yearly by the excavators in the scholarly journals "Olympische Forschungen" and "Olympia Bericht".

As the visitor enters the old Ephorate building, he sees beside the entrance a model of the Sanctuary that was made by Hans Schleif after the plans of W. Dörpfeld. It was given to the Museum of Olympia in 1931 by the German emperor Wilhelm II. Next in the display are engravings of the plain of the Sanctuary before the excavations began, photographs from the first excavations, the historic agreement of 1875 between Greece and Germany for the excavation of the Sanctuary, measuring instruments and excavation tools, photographs of the archaeologists whose names are connected with revelation of the site, many archival documents connected with the excavations, photographs of recent excavations, a list of the German scholars who have worked at Olympia and a list of the Greek Ephors as well.

MUSEUM OF THE MODERN OLYMPIC GAMES

The idea of creating a Museum of the Modern Olympic Games was that of G. Papastephanou-Provatakis (1890-1978). The Amateur Olympic Games Museum was founded in 1961 and housed in the old building of the state school of Olympia. In 1964, with the founder of the Museum as donor, the Museum came under the supervision of the Greek Olympic Committee. Then, in 1972, with funds provided by the General Secretariat of Athletics, the Museum of the Modern Olympic Games was built.

The collection contains objects connected with the modern Olympic Games, such as rare photographs, engravings, victors' honorary diplomas, posters and a unique collection of stamps, presented by G. Papastephanou, that were printed on the occasion of the various Games. Of special interest is a gold memorial medal engraved by Nikephoros Lytras for the first Olympic Games of Athens in 1896. Special reference is made to the Olympic movement before 1896 and to the efforts made to revive the Games, especially by E. Zappas (1859, 1870, 1875, 1889), up to the historic date when revival of the most important athletic institution of antiquity was finally accomplished by the French aristocrat Pierre de Coubertin.

The grave stele marking the burial place of the heart of Pierre de Coubertin, reviver of the Olympic Games, in the park of the Olympic Academy at Olympia.

The Museum of the Modern Olympic Games at Olympia.

The ceremonial arrival of the Olympic flame, established at the Games of Berlin in 1936, when it was carried in turn by 3069 runners, is represented by a series of torches.

In the forecourt of the Museum stands the case in which the heart of Pierre de Coubertin was brought to Olympia. His heart was buried in the grounds of the Olympic Academy. In the little park there is a funerary stele like those of antiquity, marking the place where the heart of the great revivalist was buried.

Gilded medal commemorating the first Olympic Games at Athens in 1896, engraved by Nikephoros Lytras.

BIBLIOGRAPHY

Ancient Sources

Homer, *Iliad, Odyssey*, translation into modern Greek by O. Komnenou-Kakridi. Zacharopoulos, Athens.

Pausanias, *Description of Greece*, Messenia and Elis, IV,V, VI, translation into modern Greek by N. Papachatzis, Ekdotike Athenon, Athens 1979.

Pindar, Olympionikai. *The Odes of Pindar*, The Loeb Classical Library, reprinted 1961.

Polybios, *History*, 4, 73 ff. and passim.

Strabo, *Geography* 8,30, pp. 350-355.

General works on the excavations, the Sanctuary, the Museums. Definitive publications

Adler F., Curtius E., Dörpfeld W., Graef P., Partsch J., Weil R., *Olympia I. Topographie und Geschichte*, 1897.

Adler F., Dörpfeld W., Graeber F., Graef P., *Olympia II. Die Baudenkmäler*, 1892-1896.

Blouet A., *Expédition Scientifique de Morée I*. Paris 1831-1838, 56 ff.

Dittenburger W., Purgold K., *Olympia V. Die Inschriften*, 1896.

Furtwängler A., *OLYMPIA IV Die Bronzen und die übrigen Kleinfunde*, 1890.

Treu G., *Olympia III. Die Bildwerke in Stein und Ton*, 1894-1897.

Other publications

Andronikos M., *Ολυμπία*, Ekdotike Athenon, Athens 2000.

Arapoyiannis X., *Ολυμπία, Η κοιτίδα των Ολυμπιακών Αγώνων*, Athens 2001.

Ashmole B.,Yalouris N., *The Sculptures of the Temple of Zeus*, London 1967.

Becatti G., *Controversie Olympiche*, Studi Miscellanei 18, 1971.

Dörpfeld W., *Alt-Olympia*, Berlin 1966 (reprint).

Ελληνική Μυθολογία (collection), Ekdotike Athenon, Athens 1986.

Herrmann H. V., *Olympia, Heiligtum und Wettkampfstätte*, Munich 1972.

Herrmann H.V., *Die Olympia - Skulpturen*, 1987.

Kaltsas, N. *Ολυμπία*, Archaeological Receipts Fund, Athens 2004 (reprint).

Kontis I. D., *Το Ιερόν της Ολυμπίας κατά τόν Δ΄ αιώνα π.Χ.*, Athens 1958.

Kyrieleis H.,(ed.). *Olympia 1875-2000, 125 Jahre Deutsche Ausgrabungen*, 2002.

Kyrieleis H.,"Zeus and Pelops in the East Pediment of the Temple of Zeus at Olympia," *The Interpretation of Architectural Sculpture in Greece and Rome*, (ed.) D. Buitron-Oliver, 1997.

Leonardos B., *Ολυμπία*, Athens 1901.

Lippold G., *Griechische Plastik*, Munich 1950.

Mallwitz A. *Olympia und seine Bauten*, Munich 1972.

Mallwitz A., Herrmann H. V., *Die Funde aus Olympia*, Athens 1980.

Olympische Forschungen, Deutsches Archäologisches Institut (1944 ff.).

Olympia Bericht, Deutsches Archäologisches Institut (1937 ff).

Säflund M. L., *The East Pediment of the Temple of Zeus at Olympia*, Göteborg, 1970.

Sinn U., "Εκθεση τών ερευνών στην Ολυμπία τής Υστερης Αρχαιότητος", *Πρωτοβυζαντινή Μεσσήνη καί Ολυμπία*, (eds. P. Themelis - B. Kontis), Athens 2002.

Vokotopoulou, I. *Αργυρά και χάλκινα έργα τέχνης*, in the series Ελληνική Τέχνη, Ekdotike Athenon, Athens 1997.

Yialouri A.,Yialouris N., *Ολυμπία, Οδηγός του Μουσείου καί του Ιερού*, Ekdotike Athenon, Athens 1998 (reprint).

Yialouris N., *Αρχαία Γλυπτά*, in the series Ελληνική Τέχνη, Ekdotike Athenon, Athens 1994-1995.

On the Olympic Games

Alexandri O. (ed) Catalogue of the Exhibition "Το Πνεύμα και το Σώμα. Οι αθλητικοί αγώνες στήν αρχαία Ελλάδα", Ministry of Culture - National Archaeological Museum, Athens 1989.

Ιστορία του Ελληνικού Έθνους, Ekdotike Athenon, vol. II, Athens 1971.

Manetti G., *Sport e giochi nell' antichità classica*, Milan 1988.

Moretti L., *Olympionikai, I vincitori negli antichi agoni olympici*, Mem.Linc. 1957.

Sinn U., *Olympia. Cult, Sport and Ancient Festival*, Princeton 2000.

Spathari E., *Το Ολυμπιακό Πνεύμα*. Adam publishers, Athens 1992.

Valavanis P. *Άθλα, Αθλητές καί Έπαθλα*, Erevnites publishers, Athens 1996.

Valavanis P., *Ιερά και αγώνες στην αρχαία Ελλάδα. Ολύμπια, Πύθια, Ίσθμια Νέμεα, Παναθήναια*.Kapon publishers, Athens 2004.

Yialouris N., (ed.) *Ιστορία τών Ολυμπιακών Αγώνων*. Ekdotike Athenon, Athens 1982.

Trianti I.,Valavanis P., *Ολυμπία και Ολυμπιακοί Αγώνες*, Athens 2004.